AF086232

Deep Purple
FIREBALL

In-depth

Laura Shenton

"Fireball is a troublesome album because, to me, you couldn't have had *Fireball* without *In Rock*, but you couldn't have *Machine Head* without *Fireball* so it sits very nicely as part of those three really good rock albums."

- Jon Lord

Deep Purple
FIREBALL

Laura Shenton

WYMER
PUBLISHING
Bedford, England

First published in 2021 by Wymer Publishing
Bedford, England www.wymerpublishing.co.uk Tel: 01234 326691
Wymer Publishing is a trading name of Wymer (UK) Ltd

Copyright © 2021 Laura Shenton / Wymer Publishing. This edition published 2021.

Print edition (fully illustrated): **ISBN: 978-1-912782-82-6**

Edited by Jerry Bloom.

The Author hereby asserts her rights to be identified
as the author of this work in accordance with sections
77 to 78 of the Copyright, Designs & Patents Act 1988.

All rights reserved. No part of this publication may be
reproduced or transmitted in any form or by any means,
electronic or mechanical, including photocopying, or any
information storage and retrieval system, without written
permission from the publisher.

This publication is sold subject to the condition that it shall not,
by way of trade or otherwise, be lent, re-sold, hired out or
otherwise circulated without the publishers' prior consent in any
form of binding or cover other than that in which it is published
and without a similar condition including this condition
being imposed on the subsequent purchaser.

eBook formatting by Coinlea.
Printed and bound in Great Britain by
CMP, Dorset.

A catalogue record for this book is available from the British Library.

Typeset by Andy Bishop / 1016 Sarpsborg
Cover design by 1016 Sarpsborg.

Contents

Preface   7

Chapter One: *Why Fireball?*   9

Chapter Two: *New Directions, New Pressures*   18

Chapter Three: *The Making Of Fireball*   35

Chapter Four: *Strange Kind Of Release Dates*   49

Chapter Five: *Bootlegging*   57

Chapter Six: *Babyface And Other Projects*   67

Chapter Seven: *Machine Head Saves The Day?*   79

Chapter Eight: *Fireball Is A Worthwhile Album*   99

Appendices   117
   Personnel
   Track Listing
   Discography
   Tour Dates

Preface

Deep Purple's *Fireball*! What an album! It's a fascinating album in terms of how it seems to significantly divide opinion between fans and even the band themselves. In writing this book, I think it's really important that I present this album objectively. In order to do that, I'll start by putting it out there where my bias sits with the album. I think it's fantastic! I feel that it was of its time and it is an enjoyable insight into what Deep Purple were doing at a time when things were really starting to take off for them. But of course, that's just my opinion and it's certainly not that which this book is framed around. For of course, the purpose of this book is to represent what *Fireball* meant to Deep Purple as individuals and in terms of their legacy overall. In such regard, this isn't going to be the story of what *I* think the album sounds like — that would be boring, I'm merely the narrator here.

Many consider that *Fireball* had many things going against it. When I put my music historian's hat on, it seems very apparent that *Fireball* was rushed in amongst what was an extremely busy period for Deep Purple: That it was not given the time and energy to be everything that it could have been — musically, commercially and in terms of how it was released and promoted. Thus, the purpose of this book is to examine those things in detail. I want to revisit the narrative surrounding *Fireball* because it is an important album in Deep Purple's discography.

As with any band, every member will have a different opinion on each of the albums they put out. As a result, I think it is tremendously important not to generalise. As someone who has no affiliation with Deep Purple or with any of their associates, in writing this book, I will be doing everything I can to quote good, reliable sources that will help to get the story of the *Fireball* album across with as much authenticity as possible. Due to this, you'll be seeing lots of quotes from vintage articles. I think they are important to document anyway because there will probably come a time when stuff like that gets harder to source.

This book is a gossip free zone. I want to present facts rather than all kinds of weird and wonderful speculations. Also, there will be nothing herein that is in the lexicon of "this song is in B minor so it probably means XYZ". Nope! Not happening! I want to present what Deep Purple experienced with *Fireball* and not what I did as one of millions of fans out there. Oh, and that reminds me, I was born in 1988 — so blummin' ages after all of this stuff happened and thus, this book is a culmination of extensive research that I intend to use objectively to offer a worthwhile narrative on, what is ultimately a very worthwhile album in *Fireball*.

Chapter One
Why Fireball?

Now, in 2021, it is probably all too easy to look back at Deep Purple's entire discography and think of *Fireball* as one of many great (or not so great, depending on your opinion) albums; there is almost this sense of inevitability of "well yeah, it's part of an amazing discography of many fascinating albums."

But what I want to do is take you back to the time of when it came out and what it meant in the context of Deep Purple's discography when it was their most recent album. *Deep Purple In Rock* had come out in 1970 and musically and commercially it had been such a big deal. But that was just one album. *Machine Head* didn't exist yet. *Burn* didn't exist yet. The fact is that Deep Purple and their fans alike had absolutely no idea what was around the corner and as a result, I think it is absolutely plausible that there may have existed a concern that *Deep Purple In Rock* was going to be a one off or a bit of a flash in the pan thing. Many people (including the members of the band themselves, which I'll get onto later) consider that *Deep Purple In Rock* was the band's breakthrough album. It is plausible that when it came to making *Fireball* after that, the pressure was on.

I'm certainly not saying that there was a problem with *Fireball* on a musical basis. Besides, that is a very subjective thing; some fans and band members will hold *Fireball* in high regard and others won't. That is inevitable. What I'm saying is that there were problems surrounding the album in terms of how it was made. Not all members of Deep Purple were happy with it. It received very mixed reviews and there seemed to be a general feeling that it was the product of a bit of a rushed job to capitalise on the success of its predecessor.

But first, some much needed context as in, we need to look at where Deep Purple was at by the time *Fireball* was being worked

Deep Purple - Fireball: In-depth

on. For context, *Fireball* was released in 1971. Deep Purple had only been going since 1968 and yet *Fireball* was their fifth studio album. That's a massive number of albums in such a short space of time and thus inevitably, loads had gone on before *Fireball*. And it is the loads that went on that matters. Seriously people, there is so much context.

Basically, before I go onto the specifics of *Fireball*, we need to go right back to 1968 when Deep Purple was a new band. The line-up known as MkI — Ritchie Blackmore on guitar, Ian Paice on drums, Jon Lord on keyboards, Nick Simper on bass and Rod Evans on vocals. In the initial days of the band, they pretty much had no association with hard rock and definitely (many would argue) no association with heavy metal. They were — and I don't wish to negate them here but in the grand scheme of things — one of many bands doing the whole psychedelic pop rock thing at the time. Their image was pretty much that of an underground band who were doing well in the States but were largely unheard of in their native country.

The *New Musical Express* reported under the title of "UK Unknowns Score US Hits" in September 1968; "Deep Purple, a British group still looking for its first chart success in its own country, is well on the way to winning a Gold Disc in America. Its 'Hush' single — released in the States on the new Tetragrammaton label — has already sold over 600,000 copies during the first four weeks of the release and is currently placed at number thirteen in the *Billboard* Hot 100. The group's first album, *Shades Of Deep Purple*, is also in the process of climbing the US album charts. In view of this unexpected success, Deep Purple has been lined up for its debut visit to America — it begins a two-month coast to coast tour at the beginning of October, which will include club and one-nighter dates as well as over twenty TV appearances. Deep Purple's second LP, as yet untitled, will be released to coincide with the visit." Jon Lord was quoted in *Melody Maker* in August 1969; "We were lucky with America. Our first record, 'Hush' was issued at exactly the right moment for the States. The top forty radio stations were beginning to lean more towards the underground and 'Hush' seemed to bridge the gap."

Shades Of Deep Purple was reviewed in *Record Mirror* in September 1968; "First LP from Deep Purple, currently riding high

Why Fireball?

in the American charts with 'Hush'. This is one of the so called "underground" groups that is not content to play solely blues. There is a lot of good music here, sometimes interspersed with sound effects and electronic noises which all adds to the performances. Listen to 'Mandrake Root' — it's a driving number with a powerful vocal from Rod Evans and stirring organ sounds from Jon Lord (who plays well throughout the LP). 'Help' is taken at a slow tempo and becomes a real plea. Try any track — they're all great, strongly recommended to all discerning pop fans. Five out of a possible five stars."

It was also reviewed in *Billboard* in the August; "An auspicious first album for this new British group. The nine cuts on this album can be taken individually or as a unit. Individually, there is Deep Purple's single, 'Hush', a languid 'Help' and a bluesy 'Hey Joe'. The classically based 'Prelude: Happiness' leads into a bright 'I'm So Glad', which concludes with the same theme."

In the same month, *Record World* advocated of the album; "The best hard rock version of 'Hey Joe' that I've heard. The vocals are not stressed, but when done, they are executed well. The disc is moving well and the single ('Hush') should be top five."

Cashbox considered in the same month; "Aimed at both teen and progressive rock markets, the quintet mixes commercialism and musicianship with finesse... Looks as though we can expect big things from Deep Purple."

The second album was *The Book Of Taliesyn*, which was released in October 1968 (US) and June 1969 (UK). That too got some pretty decent reviews (not entirely, but decent enough to suggest that Deep Purple were certainly appreciated by their, predominantly American, audience at the time).

It was reviewed in *Billboard* in December 1968; "Deep Purple scored a huge chart success with their debut album and this, this second effort, is a worthy successor. Including their hit 'Kentucky Woman', rockin' as 'River Deep, Mountain High', or employing classical musicianship as in 'Anthem', this is a together group with underground. A medley of the instrumental 'Exposition' with the Lennon-McCartney 'We Can Work It Out' is altogether a good cut."

It was reviewed in the same month in *Record World*; "Sturdy, contemporary rock based on the blues, or is it the deep purples? The

Deep Purple - Fireball: In-depth

group does unto 'Kentucky Woman', 'We Can Work It Out', 'River Deep, Mountain High' and group originals. Most of the cuts are long and really get into it."

Upon its UK release, *The Book Of Taliesyn* was reviewed by John Peel in *Disc & Music Echo* in June 1969; "This has been around for a while in the import shops — you may have noticed John Vernon Lord's excellent sleeve. All the Harvest sleeves are good, in fact, all being gatefolds or whatever you call them. Some of you may recall from 1965 or thereabouts, a record by a group called The Outlaws called 'Keep A Knocking'. The vocals weren't too amazing but there was some really lunatic guitar playing by Ritchie Blackmore who is now of Deep Purple. The group have done some fine things for Radio One and they excite when they play live — that's why I don't understand where this record went wrong. It's all too restrained somehow. Each track is well thought and well played but there is no real excitement there. Side one is the weaker side with their American hit, 'Kentucky Woman' and a poor version of 'We Can Work It Out'. Also on this side is 'Wring That Neck' which they recorded much better for a recent *Top Gear*. Side two is by far the more interesting side. It opens with 'Shield' which is very good indeed — freer and more relaxed than anything else on the LP. The second track on this side is an over-dramatic 'Anthem'. Perhaps the best thing about the group is their sense of dynamics and their ability to lead into familiar themes with unfamiliar and beautifully constructed instrumentals. This is demonstrated in 'River Deep, Mountain High', which closes this slightly disappointing album."

After the first two albums, it was pretty much the case that whilst they were doing okay in America, Deep Purple were predominantly regarded as an English group who had a reasonably modest following elsewhere.

In *New Musical Express* in September 1968, Deep Purple's 'Hush' single was advertised as "The American chart topping single."

As was reported in *Cashbox* in January 1969; "Deep Purple, the smash English rock group, is currently hitting the charts in such diverse countries as Japan, Canada, Switzerland, Australia and Mexico, on the heels of their two smash US singles ('Hush' and 'Kentucky Woman') and two bestselling albums (*Shades Of Deep*

Why Fireball?

Purple and *The Book Of Taliesyn*). At the conclusion of a successful tour in the States, prior to returning home to London, Deep Purple recorded their next single for Tetragrammaton Records, 'River Deep, Mountain High', taken from their *Taliesyn* album."

Jon Lord was quoted in *Melody Maker* in August 1969; "Part of the trouble now is that if you are not easily labelled then you have problems in England. Because England is so small and there is such a wealth of good groups, people tend to adopt a particular type of music and go to see the groups in that field. In the States it takes so long for a group to get round to a particular area that the people go along to see everything. We went to a concert that had Woody Herman, Led Zeppelin, and the Jimmy Cotton Blues Band all on the same bill."

Tetragrammaton had a reasonably high-profile reputation in the US (it was founded by music industry executives Roy Silver, Bruce Post Campbell, Marvin Deane, and comedian Bill Cosby). Problematically though, when it came to *The Book Of Taliesyn*, the chart positions were lower than expected and were not reflective of the musical acclaim with which the album was reviewed many later years. At the time though, despite having played at many key venues and festivals in America, in the UK, Deep Purple were still an underground band who played in the small clubs and college circuit.

Deep Purple just weren't managing to capture people's imagination in the UK. At the time, their UK releases were on Harvest records; the label was a division of EMI and was targeted towards a hippy audience. *Record Mirror* advocated in June 1969; "Deep Purple's Harvest debut has some interesting musical ideas and is far less samey in sound than your average underground outfit. But it is not an excitingly new production (it was made last year in fact) and while it is a great relief to hear a group that is not constantly striving for all out freak out effects and is trying instead for a little subtlety, maybe they ought to try a little more wildness, here and there, on their next LP."

When Deep Purple's third eponymous album came out, it was pretty much the same story. As with *Shades Of Deep Purple* and *The Book Of Taliesyn*, musically, there wasn't really anything that bad to say about the album but commercially, all three albums were either

Deep Purple - Fireball: In-depth

enjoyed on a small scale or went unnoticed entirely. That is to say that the reviews were pretty decent but the chart placements and sales were unremarkable.

Deep Purple's third album was reviewed in *New Musical Express* in September 1969; "Deep Purple have been through enormous policy changes since they topped the American charts with Joe South's 'Hush' and we should all be thankful for it. On this LP, the group is augmented on several numbers by strings and woodwind, but for the most part, it is all Deep Purple, inspired of course by Jon Lord's intricate and exciting organ playing, particularly on 'The Painter', which was recorded live. All the tracks are group-penned, bar Donovan's 'Lalena', which is given a jazzy treatment. The group have a tendency to be over-gimmicky at times, but then anything original and enterprising runs that risk from time to time. Other titles; 'Chasing Shadows', 'Blind', 'Fault Line', 'Why Didn't Rosemary?', 'Bird Has Flown', 'April'."

The album was also reviewed in the same month in *Record Mirror*; "One of those British groups who make it in the States but never seem to do much here (UK), Deep Purple are yet another progressive group with a competent, loud sound. They can handle ballads well, like Donovan's 'Lalena' included here, and they show a certain amount of vocal sensitivity. Instrumental work is powerful and there is a nice freaky sound on 'Fault Line'. Mostly very effective and a good album, even though it may not do too much in Britain. Cover, by Bosch, should have been in colour."

Overall, Deep Purple had achieved what many bands at the time might have been pleased with; they were well respected musically and they had a fanbase in America. However, one of the exciting things about Deep Purple, I would say, is that the founding members of the band were probably very ambitious people and thus, things certainly didn't seem to be going in a direction that was to the liking of Ritchie Blackmore.

He was quoted in *The Guardian* in April 2015; "I saw Ian (Paice) with another band in Hamburg in 1967 and I said, 'When I get something, I'll let you know.' When this Purple thing came up, I said 'Right, we've got something here' — we had a millionaire backer — it's very hard to start without financial backing. He just wanted

Why Fireball?

a very good group. As far as Chris Curtis (from the Searchers) was concerned, Jon was the best organist he knew and I was the best guitarist. But once we all got together, he kind of fell out. I told Jon about Ian and then we got the other two: Jon knew Nick (Simper) and I knew Rod (Evans) the singer. We were all living in one big mansion in England, which we used to rehearse in. There were a lot of things happening there, psychic phenomena. For the first few years, Purple had no direction whatsoever. If anything, we used to follow what Jon wanted to do, which was okay because nobody else had any ideas."

During the days of touring America on the back of the 'Hush' single, Deep Purple still had a lack of direction in terms of where they were going to go with it. Blackmore was quoted in the same interview as he elaborated on the situation; "Jeff Wald (Mr Helen Reddy) was our manager on the road and we did a lot of gigs that didn't mean anything. They were ballrooms, they weren't on the circuit to make it. We'd be playing around, headlining all the wrong places. Nobody knew where to put us. We played with Cream at the Hollywood Bowl, but they never really knew who we were."

Blackmore said in *Sounds* in February 1974 as he described what the general motive was in the MkI days of Deep Purple; "We were feeling so happy to be playing together and happy to be on a wage, it meant the world to us. We thought it would only last six months and the guy who backed us would get fed up and say 'that's it' and we'd be back in Germany. But it so happened that 'Hush' caught on and went into the charts and we went off to America and that was the beginning. We'd a hard time proving to the Americans that we weren't a teenybop band because that single was slightly in a teeny vein. And every night people came saying, 'oh, I thought you were a teenybop band' and in the end it got to the point of, 'oh fuck, leave it out'."

Jon Lord told *Melody Maker* in March 1971; "It was puzzling to me and the others! There was just a lack of direction. The first three albums were pleasant, but directionless. Nobody knew quite what on earth the group was doing."

After three albums that, as Blackmore and Lord perhaps saw it, meandered around a lack of focus and did reasonably okay but weren't that much of a big deal, it was time for a line-up change that saw Rod Evans and Nick Simper replaced by Ian Gillan and Roger Glover.

Ian Paice said in *Modern Drummer* in October 2014; "Thinking musically means you have to adapt to every piece you're playing. 'Hush', which was a big hit, was a samba beat. Now, if you don't have that feel down, then the song doesn't work. The fact that it had a nice avant-garde free-form organ solo at the end meant that I could do other things, but it was still within that rhythm. The limitations of the first incarnation of Deep Purple included Rod Evans' voice. He was a pretty good balladeer, but he wasn't a great rock 'n' roll singer. We were held back on certain things that we were edging towards, but we could never quite get there because Rod's voice wasn't made for that. When we acquired Ian Gillan and Roger Glover in 1969, all the ideas that had never quite come to fruition now began to blossom. You say the drumming style changed — well, it had to, because the music being created was different."

Ritchie Blackmore said in *Disc & Music Echo* in March 1972; "Mick Underwood told me about Ian Gillan and he looked like Jim Morrison so we said we'll have him."

Blackmore was also quoted on the matter in *Sounds* in February 1974; "I knew a guy who played for a band called Quatermass. I phoned him up and asked him if he knew any singers... I saw Ian (Gillan) and was knocked out. And Ian Paice was knocked out with Roger Glover and we took him as well." The Mk1 line-up of Deep Purple did their last gig at the Top Rank in Cardiff on 4th July 1969.

On balance, it would probably be quite an overstatement to say that things were going wrong for Deep Purple during the days of the MkI line-up. It's just that essentially, MkII signified a substantial change in the way that the band approached the music.

As Roger Glover was quoted in *OnMilwaukee* in October 2019; "I would disagree that Deep Purple stumbled at the beginning. After all, they put out three albums and a couple of charting singles in eighteen months. But it's true that many of the songs were covers. I think it's more accurate to say they were a band in search of an identity. The difference was that Ian (Gillan) and I immediately started writing new material, and the resulting album, *In Rock*, was entirely made up of original songs. I hesitate to analyse it too much,

Why Fireball?

but I must point out that the band was made up of stellar musicians. Ian Paice was, and is, a fabulous drummer. Jon Lord and Ritchie Blackmore were both classically trained players, and they brought that element to the mix. I couldn't believe how good everyone was. I had never played with people like that! It was a fragile connection, as these things often are, but I think their virtuosity as musicians was one of the keys to our success."

Chapter Two

New Directions, New Pressures

With the MkII line-up of Deep Purple consisting of Blackmore, Lord, Paice, Gillan and Glover, there was scope to take the band in a new and innovative direction. One of the most distinctive MkII features is that their songs portray an exciting sense of drama and atmosphere. The intense drumming from Paice, the heavy and distinctive riffs from Blackmore and Lord all underscored with Glover's bass playing and new ideas, and of course, Gillan's charismatic vocals. That is to say that with Ian Gillan and Roger Glover joining the three founding members, the scope was there to launch the band into a new direction that would see them make their mark in the early seventies and indeed beyond. Jon Lord was quoted in *Melody Maker* in March 1971 as he explained what a turning point it was when Roger Glover and Ian Gillan joined Deep Purple to make up what would be the MkII band; "There was a tremendous upswing and renaissance when they joined."

By thinking commercially, Ritchie Blackmore in particular was already very instrumental in identifying what needed to be done to move forward — and that's where the first song recorded by MkII comes into the picture, 'Hallelujah'.

Blackmore told *Record Mirror* in September 1969; "Quite honestly, we need to have a commercial record in Britain. We're going to the States for between six months and a year, but that would mean we'd be away so long. We want to be known in England so we've come out very much on the commercial side with the new record. 'Hallelujah' is an in between sort of thing. Something of what we normally do, and also the commercial influence. Really, you have to think commercially to be able to live. There's no point in being a fantastic musician if you're starving to death. I sometimes get fed up burning from the looks some of the orchestra were giving me. You know, the usual kind of 'who do these long-haired freaks think they are?' looks. And there was a lot of problems with the sound balance. Finally, I had to rent a Hammond organ which could play quieter than my own one. Then on Tuesday rehearsal, things began to click a bit better. One of the violinists behind me was really getting into it and muttering 'yeah, far out' and such like to me. Lawrence Foster, the conductor, was really great and worked hard to whip everything into shape. And at the end of *Concerto*, when I asked the orchestra to rise and take a bow, well, they almost fainted. I don't suppose they expected me to know the correct "classical" etiquette."

In Ian Gillan's 1993 autobiography, *Child In Time*, he recalled a moment of tremendous friction between Deep Purple and the orchestra when preparing for the first run of the concerto at London's Royal Albert Hall; "The first rehearsal with the orchestra and the band ended with emotions running high, (managers) John (Coletta) and Tony (Edwards) could be seen sitting in the auditorium, heads deep in hands, while a female cellist stood up and shouted something about not playing with second-rate Beatles, only to be told by Malcolm (Arnold, conductor) not to be so silly. Then there was another very lacklustre effort by the Royal Philharmonic Orchestra which prompted our conductor to stop all the resentment in a no-nonsense manner that quite shocked us. Increasingly irritated by their attitude, halfway through the first movement, he rapped his baton furiously, raised his hands in the air and said words to the effect of 'I don't know what you think you're doing. You're supposed to be the finest orchestra in Britain, and you're playing like a bunch of cunts. Quite frankly, with the way it's going, you're not fit to be on stage with these guys, so pick yourself up and lets hear some bollocks'."

Jon Lord told *Melody Maker* in August 1969; "Pop music has grown up. There is now a big audience for the so-called uncommercial groups. The music has started to mean something and good musicians are to be found in abundance in the pop field. And the audiences have caught up although the great beast that sells it to the public hasn't climbed up the hill yet. If you think about it, you will realise that all the groups playing something worthwhile have been around for quite a time and the guys are all twenty-four or twenty-five. It is

New Directions, New Pressures

with the whole business — conforming to the rules and going into the studio to make hit records."

Ian Gillan's perspective on the situation pretty much sums up how well 'Hallelujah' didn't fare as he was quoted in *New Musical Express* in March 1971; "The band had three albums and five singles out in America when I joined but they had, had absolutely nothing in the way of hits in this country (UK) at all. We did a single called 'Hallelujah' which did nothing. It was a silly thing to do because none of us really knew each other. We were going out for about fifty pounds a night when things started to build up. When we really started writing and got into a sort of groove together it got better for us."

The next stop of the journey was in the form of *Concerto For Group And Orchestra* in 1969. Some people, including Deep Purple themselves, considered that the concerto wasn't reflective of the direction that the band ultimately needed and indeed wanted to go in.

Blackmore said in *Disc & Music Echo* in September 1970; "I'm getting a bit tired of the things we're doing with classical orchestras. Even Jon's getting fed-up with it now. We just want to be a rock band."

In fairness to Jon Lord though and what he wanted to create at the time, he was quoted in *New Musical Express* in March 1971; "I got slammed by various people for trying to put rock music above its station by doing the concerto and the *Gemini Suite* but I wasn't trying to elevate pop in any way. I was just trying to create a new level for the purposes of enjoyment. I was just saying 'here's an electric guitar and here's a violin, isn't it nice?' Preconception is a terrible beast, it destroys so many people. All you've got to do is go and open your ears. Even if one member of a 12,000-strong audience digs it, you've achieved something. The first purpose of music is to entertain."

In such regard, with Lord's best intentions for the concerto being what they were, it's a shame that it was met with an amount of scorn. That said, there was sufficient interest for a repeat performance at the Hollywood Bowl on 25th August 1970 with the Los Angeles Philharmonic Orchestra conducted by Lawrence Foster. Lord told the *New Musical Express* in September 1970; "I felt that my back wa

New Directions, New Pressures

happening because their musicianship has improved. What was the thing that turned people on to modern jazz? I can tell you; it was guys pushing their instruments to the limit and saying it all in music. That has now gone into the pop field. Improvisation is the order of the day and people who, a few years ago, condemned all pop music are now finding nice things in it... People will say we're doing it because other groups have done it, but in fact I had the idea five years ago — but I've never been with a group I thought could do it — until now. It won't be a case of doing a pop version of suitable classical themes. I am writing the whole lot from scratch. We will be doing a concerto. I know it sounds pretentious, but the last thing we want to be is pretentious or edifying. I want people to have fun. We will be working with an eighty-five-piece symphony orchestra conducted by Malcolm Arnold and, after preliminary meetings, I feel our only real problem will be getting the right balance between group and orchestra."

The reviews for *Concerto For Group And Orchestra* were very mixed. They ranged from impressed to disparaging. In June 1970, *Rolling Stone* gave it a particularly harsh review; "This is one of the dullest attempts yet at the fusion of rock and the European classical tradition. Lest you think Malcolm Arnold and the Royal Philharmonic Orchestra and something like the New York Philharmonic and Leonard Bernstein, you should know that they mainly deal in movie soundtracks (*Lawrence Of Arabia*) and related garbage. Composer of the "concerto", Purple organist, Jon Lord says of the piece that it is 'still only a beginning.' God help us. England hasn't given the world a composer since Händel died, and he was German."

New Musical Express advocated of *Concerto For Group And Orchestra* in December 1969; "The evening was fun and the album can't hope to capture the incredible atmosphere but to the thousands who loved the music, this very fine LP will be a must."

Blackmore told *Record Mirror* in September 1969; "The concert is purely a gimmick! The idea comes from our organist Jon Lord. He's always wanted to play with a symphony orchestra."

He also said in June 1970 in *Disc & Music Echo*; "I didn't really enjoy the thing we did with the orchestra. But I was happy for Jon Lord. We don't write together now like we used to, but we're not growing apart musically. We both like each other's stuff. He's happy now he's done his concerto and happy just to play with the band."

Concerto was reviewed in *Record Mirror* in October 1969; "If the audience reaction was anything to go by, the Deep Purple concert with the Royal Philharmonic Orchestra was a resounding success. And it was. The difficulty of welding classical music with any other form of music is that the finished article stands or falls by the classical standards. Organist with Deep Purple, Jon Lord had a classical training and knows what it's about. Although his work, *Concerto For Group And Orchestra*, might not have pleased the classical pundits from a musical level, it certainly pleased the Deep Purple fans. In the first movement, the group and the orchestra weren't together. But this was intentional, as Jon's idea was to show them as antagonists. The orchestra set the theme and Deep Purple took over with Ritchie Blackmore improvising at double tempo. The next two movements showed both factions getting together and responding to each other. Deep Purple were like a section of the orchestra. The second movement opened with a sombre statement from the basses and trombones with French horns before going into a 6/8 vocal with group and string accompaniment. A lengthy section with sensitive scoring and the woodwinds giving an air of tranquillity. The third movement had a sort of cowboy lope to it and included a lengthy drum solo from Ian Paice. A crash-bang-wallop end to a fine achievement. If you had knowledge of classical music you might have found the concerto a little derivative. If you had gone with an open mind, I'm sure you would have enjoyed it no end. Let's hope this isn't just a one-shot of pop and classical fusions. At the end of the first half, Deep Purple showed they're not another of these noisy groups — their dynamics were a delight to hear."

Brilliant review! I think it's actually the fairest one as in, it alludes to the limitations of the project but also, the reviewer speaks highly of what went right. Of course, playing with orchestras wasn't ultimately the direction that, on the whole, Deep Purple wanted to go in but that's certainly not to say that *Concerto For Group And Orchestra* is without its merits.

In *Rolling Stone* in May 1972, Lester Bangs reported that, in his opinion at least, Deep Purple had been kind of floundering for a while; "I just don't understand, as Ann-Margret once sang, why an exciting band like Deep Purple, who consistently hit the top of the charts in Merrie Olde and have taken Europe by storm, remain a comparatively unknown quantity to American audiences. Especially when said audiences have wholeheartedly embraced bands with similar musical aims and not one more ampere of excitement. It's a shame, but Deep Purple themselves are at least partially to blame. Their first two American albums on Tetragrammaton were mostly uninspired, despite some good cover versions of songs like 'I'm So Glad' and 'Hush'. The basic problem seemed to be that the group hadn't really learned to write yet, so the covers were the best way to grow without losing the audience. Except that no self-respecting late-Sixties rock band wants to put out an album with nothing but covers on it, so we were left with a bunch of boring originals, half of them instrumental. When, that is, they weren't indulging in long "improvisational" forays such as their first album's bolero rendition of 'Hey Joe'. Jon Lord was the main culprit here, having a background of extensive formal keyboard training which tended to make his solos at least a bit Emersonic and at most positively pompous. The pretentious side of Deep Purple found its fullest expression in their first album for Warner's, *Concerto For Group And Orchestra*, written by Lord and performed with the aid of Malcolm Arnold and the Royal Philharmonic Orchestra. It was an atrocity. A "movement" would begin with a few minutes of "symphonic" mush, then abruptly the orchestra would stop and the band would start to play, build until you thought they were just about to really start cooking, and then — whoosh — drowned in string sections again. A recent Lord-Arnold collaboration on Capitol called *Gemini Suite* was just more of the same miscegenation."

Ultimately, the concerto was worthwhile in terms of how it drew the media's attention to Deep Purple. As Ian Gillan described it in his autobiography; "The audience didn't know when to applaud or if to dance or sit but, to give praise where it is due, it was a stunning success for Jon and did Purple no harm at all."

Essentially though, it wasn't quite what everyone had in mind as a long term aspiration for the band. Blackmore recalled in March 1972 in *Disc & Music Echo*; "The classical thing got completely out

Deep Purple - Fireball: In-depth

of hand. We'd turn up to gigs and people would say 'where's your orchestra?' I think Jon realises now he doesn't really want to do that anymore, he may go back to it in a couple of year's time but I think he'll end up doing film music."

Even as the main instigator of the project, Jon Lord told *Record Mirror* in October 1970 as he discussed the limitations of the concerto and how he was happy to be going in a more heavy rock based direction with Deep Purple; "It drew attention to us at a time when we needed attention but we never expected it to label us "that group who play with orchestras" because we have always basically been a rock group. One of the problems with mixed-media is that you never really get total co-operation from the musicians you are mixing your media with because they never seem prepared to go halfway in meeting the musician. The other problem is that it became a kind of musical cult instead of a musical experiment on a different level. I'm very much into what the group are doing now and I think that our policy of gigging almost anywhere in the past six months up and down the country has really got through. What we are doing now has always been at the root of our music and I think the introduction of Ian Gillan and Roger Glover really gave us the guts to stand by our own musical convictions."

In his autobiography, Ian Gillan recalled (as he saw it), Ritchie Blackmore's frustration at the orchestral image Deep Purple had acquired due to the concerto; "Once in particular at a gig in Folkestone, we'd pulled into town for an appearance at the Lees Cliff Hotel to see posters saying 'Deep Purple in concert with the so-and-so silver band' — Ritchie took one look at it and went berserk, ranting on about the concerto becoming a millstone around our neck, it was extremely embarrassing because the promoter, like others, had heard all about the Albert Hall show and presumed that was how we liked to do things."

All that said though, as Gillan continued, "Thanks to *Concerto*, we were certainly better known, so our pay went up as we went into 1970, either headlining or at least taking second place to bands like Canned Heat."

With all of the latter in mind, this is where the story of *Fireball* comes into play as in, after so much experimentation and meandering,

New Directions, New Pressures

it was *In Rock* that really put Deep Purple on the map both musically and in terms of getting a strong extent of commercial attention. After years of being (and probably feeling like) a directionless underground band, *In Rock* really got things moving for Deep Purple. Ian Gillan said to *Melody Maker* in June 1970; "It was in Dundee that I heard the album had gone into the charts. We were having lunch when Tony Edwards announced it and, after so many years of struggle and disappointment, I just burst into tears. Within one year everything had changed, and now it all seemed, for once, so very simple."

Jon Lord said in an interview of his that featured posthumously in the Drew Thompson produced 2014 documentary, *Deep Purple: Made In Japan*; "There we are, really searching for an identity, and that search goes on pretty much through the first three (studio) albums."

Ian Paice said in his interview that featured in the same documentary; "(*In Rock*) became a phenomenon in the British charts. I mean it was in the top ten for over a year. It hit a chord with the British youth and Europe."

In the 1991 Paul Justman directed documentary, *Deep Purple: Heavy Metal Pioneers*, Ian Paice said; "It wasn't any one song, it was the whole album came out in a much harder vein than even we could have imagined it would have been. Every track on that album is a powerful statement about one thing or another, whether it had been a lyrical statement, anti-drugs or a musical statement with the virtuosity in the band."

In the same documentary, Roger Glover said; "Ritchie said that if it's not exciting or dramatic, it doesn't belong on the album."

As was reported by Mark Plummer in *Melody Maker* in August 1970, "Since their new album, *Deep Purple In Rock*, reached the shops and started selling, the group feel they have found an identity. The classical group tag they have been landed with does not really fit them."

Ritchie Blackmore was quoted in the same feature; "The classical thing is dead and buried as far as we are concerned," to which Ian Gillan added; "People who think we have a classical influence are not aware of what we are doing. It was just one gig that gave us a hell of a lot of publicity, and something that happened in the past. Rock is

Deep Purple - Fireball: In-depth

really what we are into."

In Rock was a statement of intent and a statement of identity for Deep Purple. The reporter in *Disc & Music Echo* gave a good summary of what *In Rock* meant to the band in June 1970; "Deep Purple are exciting, musically talented, and the highest paid group among those who haven't had hit singles or albums. They have done successful tours of America and their thing with the classical orchestra at the Albert Hall last year is generally considered to be the most successful of its kind. Really, they should be bigger than they are. And that is why their new album, *Deep Purple In Rock* and the separate single 'Black Night' are so important to them. The album is the first one that really features Ian Gillan and bass-player Roger Glover, although the two former members of Episode Six have been with Deep Purple since last July. It is also the nearest album to what they are like."

Ritchie Blackmore told *Sounds* in February 1974; "*In Rock* was, to me, the first LP."

Jon Lord said in *Melody Maker* in March 1971; "We made a conscious effort to stop and think about writing material we all understood. And the result was *Deep Purple In Rock*, which was really our stage act. That was the turning point. And the point is — we do believe in what we are doing together."

'Black Night' was reviewed in *New Musical Express* in June 1970; "One of those complex, deep thinking progressive groups who necessarily take a little time to get their musical message across — which is why Purple has fared so well with albums. To condense all they have to offer in three minutes is asking a lot. But the boys have well nigh succeeded with this heavy rocker."

Also in June 1970, *Record Mirror* reviewed it; "Nice repetitive riff here, an instrumental at first. (The) group has the right sort of following to click, even if this track seems to lack something. Musicianly (sic)."

In Rock was a bit of a double-edged sword in terms of how it performed in the charts. The album's sales were stratospheric compared to how all of Deep Purple's MkI albums had performed. *In Rock* signified Deep Purple getting the attention they wanted (and arguably deserved) in their native UK where it got to number four

New Directions, New Pressures

in the chart but equally, where MkI had been successful in America before, *In Rock* only got to 143 in the US chart. This was largely due to the problems that arose following the demise of Tetragrammaton. Warner Bros. — who inherited the band through acquisition of Tetragrammaton's liquidation — were initially unsure about the type of band Deep Purple was or how they should be marketed.

It was reported in *New Musical Express* in May 1970; "When Jimi Hendrix broke up his Experience and went back to America, a huge gap was left in Britain. On-stage excitement was hard to find. But on Monday night, at the Queen Elizabeth Hall, excitement returned in the shape of Deep Purple. They played two shows to capacity audiences and tore the place apart with their musicianship and controlled volume — which ranged from very gentle to ear-splitting level. Opening with two numbers from the forthcoming *Deep Purple In Rock* LP, 'Speed King' and 'Child In Time', vocalist Ian Gillan's screaming vibrato voice was all but drowned out by the power of the instruments, but this is the only criticism one can find in their act, Gillan's voice is, in fact, really a fifth instrument in the group. Drummer, Ian Paice and bass player Roger Glover then laid the riff for an old Purple favourite, 'Wring That Neck', which featured some brilliant organ playing from Jon Lord and his multi-toned Hammond and some fine guitar work from Ritchie Blackmore. Blackmore's technical brilliance is of the quality you wouldn't believe if you didn't actually see it. Leaping, staggering and lurching all over the half of the stage which he controls, Ritchie's showmanship almost outclassed his musicianship. The closing number, another old album track 'Mandrake Root', featured vocalist Ian Gillan on conga drums. 'Mandrake' built into a deafening strobe-lighted climax after which the only thing the group could possibly do would be to wreck their instruments. Paice kicked his drums all over the stage and Blackmore physically toppled two six-foot speaker columns over on top of his discarded guitar. It took the audience about thirty seconds to recover from their state of limp shock before giving Deep Purple a much-deserved standing ovation."

Melody Maker reviewed *In Rock* in June 1970; "A stunningly good album from a group that proves several things on it. 1) That rock, given a fresh stab and alert material, is still one of the most

Deep Purple - Fireball: In-depth

rewarding areas of contemporary music. 2) That it need not be all frenzy, but can also reach out and project a message when it's cool and wistful. 3) That Ritchie Blackmore is not merely a fast guitarist, but one with immense style and presence. The recording quality here is so good that, perhaps for the first time, the textures of some fine instrumentalists, and let's not forget a powerful singer, are given the correct emphasis. On 'Child In Time' Ian Gillan's blistering vocal, moralising in too general terms about the state of things, is matched only in style by Blackmore's masterly guitar work which is completely in context. His sympathy with the mood of each work throughout this album is quite remarkable. Jon Lord's exciting work at the organ is another strength and as a unit they are perfectly integrated. A magnificent album, which no enthusiast of today's music dare miss."

The album was reviewed in *Disc & Music Echo* in the same month; "*Deep Purple In Rock*, rock being the operative word. Ritchie Blackmore's gutsy guitar tears its way through the album, dominating it, and Jon Lord keeps very much to the role of backing musician. When he does contribute his delicate and thoughtful pieces, he uplifts what is generally a very fine sound. Their wild 'Speed King' is a conglomeration of early rock 'n' roll lyrics strung together and is in line with other groups looking back to their roots. At times the album is "Nice-ish" but on the whole, a monster album and very exciting."

This review in particular certainly gets across what the spirit of *In Rock* is. Many would probably disagree though, with the comment that suggests that Jon Lord is merely a backing musician! Everyone in that band made it as great as it was.

The content on *In Rock* came about largely on the basis of the excitement and enthusiasm within the band at the time. Jam sessions would often merge into ideas that stuck and were ultimately worked into songs. Usually one person would put an idea forward and the rest of the band would join in. The organic nature of the writing process was such that it was decided that all band members would be given equal credit on every song. This continued to be the case until the MkIII line-up a few years later.

Roger Glover in particular, was a creative asset; he was often

New Directions, New Pressures

coming up with ideas and his talents were able to shine in a way that hadn't been possible for him in Episode Six. Ritchie Blackmore told *Disc & Music Echo* in June 1970; "Ian is better than the other singer and Roger has more ideas than the bass player we had before. And this new album is a lot better than the previous ones. I've always been disappointed with our albums. The first one was a good attempt for a first. But people have always said 'It's not you' — we've always tried to be too flash on our records but basically we are an exciting band. When I play on stage I like to get people into a kind of party thing. People want to enjoy themselves. We're serious about the music but we do a lot of showmanship and people think, because of that, that it's suspect. They say, 'what is he leaping around for?' — but I like to leap around. The thing is that when you're making a record there is no point in leaping around for the benefit of the engineer so the albums have lacked something. I don't think we'd want to do a live one because they get messy, like *The Who Live At Leeds*, That's not half as good as they usually are on record. Our new one is certainly the nearest to what we are like on stage. And it's the first to represent the band as it is now. It's much harder, raucous and exciting. That is what we are trying to get across, rather than musical ability. It's hard and simple. I hate the last three LPs. I think bands should be exciting live. There are so many groups going round with a hidden message — and they are so boring."

Blackmore said in March 1972 in *Disc & Music Echo*; "With Ian (Gillan), he can't write a song straight out, he has to write over the framework we've already written and laid down and although that's difficult for him we've found that's the best way to work. It had to start from the beginning like that or we'd never have got anywhere at all, and I still think the first songs we did were the best."

Ian Gillan explained to *Kerrang!* in August 1982; "I start with noises, percussive sounds, I start singing gibberish. Then, when I've got some kind of phrase structure and the metre of the verse worked out, I do a lot of notation and start on the subject matter. When that's decided I just write about a page of a story to get the ideas out, the colour and the pictures, then go back to my notes on the metre and the phrasing and start looking for musical words because you can't take poetry and short stories and put them to music. It doesn't work."

Deep Purple - Fireball: In-depth

On the 25th Anniversary edition of *Fireball* released in 1996, Roger Glover wrote for the liner notes; "Typically we would record the backing tracks all together and then Jon and Ritchie would overdub their solos and Ian Gillan would do his vocals (on this album the lyrics were pretty much all his)."

Glover told *New Musical Express* in February 1972; "Officially it's a five-way split when we write, but different people contribute different things to different songs. We know who wrote what, but I don't think it's apparent to the listener. For example, *Fireball* was written mainly by Ritchie, Jon and Ian. The basic ideas usually stem from Ritchie and myself. On the new album (*Machine Head*, which was to be released in March 1972) I got most of my ideas during the four weeks off, just because I was able to take time off and listen to some music and also drive around in my car and relax. On the lyrics side, sometimes Ian Gillan will do them on his own, or we'll get together. With one particular track on the new album, 'Smoke On The Water', that particular phrase just came to me. My first thought was to write it myself as a folk song. I mentioned the idea to Ian, and no more was said until we came to write the lyrics of a song in the studio. So that's how that number came about. Sometimes I feel I'd like more credit for some of the stuff I do, but the decision to split it five ways was made ages ago before *Deep Purple In Rock*. That's because our music is basically the result of a jam session. I think it avoids friction this way, though I can't say it won't in the future. As soon as money comes into it, people change. Some for the better — some for the worse."

Ritchie Blackmore was interviewed in April 2015 in *The Guardian* and said; "I did most of the riffs and progressions because, basically, we had so many arguments in the first two years of Purple, and I was sick of it, so I said let's split it five ways, because everyone was bickering about 'I wrote that one note' (and) 'Include this song, which is a bunch of rubbish, but I wrote it' — every band goes through that. There's one thing today we haven't got over with modern technology. We haven't found a way to fashion a computer to take the information and tell you who's written the song. That would be very nice. People said to me, 'You were silly to split it five ways for most of it' but I said, 'Purple wouldn't have been together

New Directions, New Pressures

at all if I hadn't done that' because they were very strong-minded people. It would have died out in 1970 if I hadn't done that."

In Rock was recorded at three different studios; IBC, De Lane Lea and Abbey Road. It was at De Lane Lea that Deep Purple first worked with Martin Birch, where he was the in-house engineer and worked as the assistant to Barry Ainsworth, who had engineered the first three Derek Lawrence produced Purple albums. Birch would go on to work in the studio with them as their right hand man until Deep Purple's initial breakup in 1976.

The entire recording process was done sporadically between October 1969 through to April 1970 and the whole project ultimately revolved around their packed tour schedule (it was really something in terms of volume of gigs and the travelling required. Be sure to take a look at this in the appendices of this book for a full extent of context).

The intense tour schedule made sense in terms of striking while the iron was hot, what with *Concerto For Group And Orchestra* having propelled Deep Purple further into the public eye. Also, the sheer number of gigs played were an excellent opportunity for the band to recoup some money (they were still in debt at the time) and tighten up material for what would be recorded on the album that came to be known as *In Rock*. Gillan and Glover were not new to touring. Glover told *Sounds* in March 1976; "Before Deep Purple I had been on the road since 1965 professionally, that's a fair while."

As new as the accelerated touring patterns may have been to Deep Purple as a whole unit by the point of *In Rock*, at the end of the day, all five band members were seasoned professionals who had been working their way up in the music business for years prior to *In Rock* taking off in the way that it did.

As was reported in *Rolling Stone* in June 1973; "*In Rock* (was) the precise representation of second-generation Deep Purple and, in the eyes of many, the definitive heavy-metal masterwork. For the most part ignored in the US, the LP was a smash throughout Europe and insured the band's comeback. Deep Purple themselves still consider *In Rock* their best effort to date."

Ritchie Blackmore said in April 2015; "Why we thought we had to change singers was because of Robert Plant. We were playing at

Deep Purple - Fireball: In-depth

Mother's in Birmingham and Robert got up to sing with Terry Reid. We thought, Christ almighty! He was so dynamic. And the next two weeks we were looking for a singer, people who had Robert Plant's dynamic approach. So it was thanks to him. Zeppelin — I liked their hard approach when they came out and did 'Whole Lotta Love'. I immediately tuned in with that type of style because before when we were fiddling around with orchestras, I thought 'something's wrong; I'm not giving all that I can' — thanks to them for the inspiration. They got it from Jeff Beck, who got it from the Small Faces."

And in an interview done by Neil Jeffries in September 1995, originally published in *More Black Than Purple*: "We were a rock band. I couldn't understand why we kept playing with orchestras. It started to get up my nose. The first thing was a novelty, a band playing with an orchestra. I didn't think it was particularly good but we pulled it off. Then Jon wrote another one (*Gemini Suite*), and they wanted us to do it again. I went, 'No, no. I'm not getting involved again. I'm in a rock 'n' roll band,' I said, 'Jon, we should make a rock 'n' roll record for people in parties. It should be non-stop, hard-hitting rock 'n' roll.' I was impressed with what Zeppelin did, and I wanted to do that kind of stuff, and if it doesn't take off we'll go and play with orchestras the rest of our lives. So we did it, and it was *Deep Purple In Rock*, which, luckily, took off. We'd purposely made it so it hammered along every song, there was no lull. I was very pleased with it because I never wanted to work with an orchestra again."

In Rock was reflective of a band making a conscious decision to create a product with good commercial potential. Ritchie Blackmore was quoted in May 1971 in *Record Mirror*; "Of course we consider our market and the people who come to listen to us. In that sense we make concessions and I just don't believe in all this crap about "doing your own thing" — I did my own thing for a while some two years ago and I starved. All the musicians and heads came in and said, 'great guitar man' and I still starved. It is more satisfying to me and most other musicians to have people listen and I get a personal kick out of creating music which generates an exciting atmosphere. Pete Townsend made the point that there is no point progressing unless you take the people with you! There is a whole lot of hypocrisy and

New Directions, New Pressures

snobbery connected with certain groups in some minds who have given us stick for being overtly commercial. We enjoy what we do and we would never release anything we did not want to be associated with. If we release records which appeal to several million instead of a few hundred, I'm not about to apologise for it. We release singles and hope they are hits because we think it is important to try and reach as many people as possible — those who might not ordinarily buy the album. We do *Top Of The Pops* because if you are going to release a single it is the one show which really counts. Not to do it is to cut your own throat."

Roger Glover said in *New Musical Express* in June 1971; "I'm very proud of *In Rock*. We knew it was going to sell well because we'd done six months of concerts and we knew it would do well, but no one expected it to last this long."

With a higher public profile came, presumably, more obligation to comply to a few commercial commitments that perhaps wouldn't have been their first choice. As Ian Gillan told *Melody Maker* in August 1970; "We haven't wanted to do television before, with all the hassles and three minute spots playing to backing tracks. But the *Southbank* thing was great, we got top billing above Blue Mink and the Settlers. The other groups played to backing tracks but we took all our gear and played live. Of course, as usual, the audience was made up of a lot of older people. Anyway, we played 'Child In Time', which is a pretty quiet one for us. It was funny — when we finished we said we were going to do a loud one, and half the audience walked out. Still, we were pleased to do it. The producer, Brian Izzard, gave us a lot of freedom and a half hour set, we didn't give a monkey about the people who walked out."

In the same interview, Ritchie Blackmore was quoted; "The audiences clap when they're told to, and it seems that the TV people are frightened of inviting hip audiences — maybe they think they will strip off or something."

As was reported in *New Musical Express* in June 1971; "Still selling very strongly, *In Rock* has notched up British sales of close to 150,000 and has appeared in multitudinous charts right round the world. For Deep Purple, it was, as other members of the group have explained in earlier interviews, a turning point for Deep Purple."

Deep Purple - Fireball: In-depth

Brilliant! With *In Rock*, Deep Purple had cracked it in terms of finally, after all that hard work, getting some much-deserved success. And this is where some of the challenges surrounding *Fireball* come into the frame as in, it seems to be that there was suddenly this shared feeling among everyone in the band that went something along the lines of "shit! We've got to follow *that* up now!"

Roger Glover said in the Drew Thompson produced 2014 documentary, *Deep Purple: Made In Japan*; "*In Rock* stayed in the charts for over a year, a big success to follow. There was a feeling of, 'well what do we do next? How do we top that?'."

Ian Paice said in *Rolling Stone* in June 1973; "The album (*In Rock*) came quite easily for us. The hardest thing about it was following it up. We were working so much due to the success that when we tried to do the next album, *Fireball*, we realised we had no ideas whatsoever. *Fireball* turned out to be a bit of a 'Let's hope we've got an album's worth here' type of thing."

Roger Glover was quoted in *Uncut* in November 2015 as he explained the pressure that was on them after the success of *In Rock*; "We were following up a big success and you can't be unaware of that. We went down to a big old house, The Hermitage, in north Devon to write."

Not much got done though and the productivity of that period was certainly questionable. In the same feature, Ian Gillan was quoted of the writing; "That didn't last very long. Pranks, axes through doors, that sort of thing. I'm not sure what got done. We drank a lot of cider," to which Glover elaborated; "It was Ritchie wielding the axe and it was through my door. He wanted to borrow a crucifix because he was having a séance. I didn't want anything to do with it. I was in bed reading my book, and the next thing I knew, an axe came through my door and there was Ritchie. He's a great practical joker, but I thought he went a little too far. We'd been on the road about a year, and a little bit of drink came into it. I can't remember what we wrote there apart from 'Strange Kind Of Woman'." Ah yes, the busy touring and strains of the rock 'n' roll lifestyle were certainly a factor when after the success of *In Rock*, it was time to make *Fireball*.

Chapter Three
The Making Of Fireball

Despite the massive success that Deep Purple had with *In Rock*, it sometimes leaves one wondering if they were really able to enjoy it. Some consider that Ian Gillan and Ritchie Blackmore had friction and ego conflicts even as early on in the band as not long after *In Rock* had been made. We'll never really know because we weren't there but it is certainly plausible as in, Deep Purple certainly consisted of strong personalities. Ian Gillan offered his perspective in his autobiography; "The main problem in the band had become centred on me and Ritchie, and because he was the more forceful of us, and better able to catch the attention of management, I was seen as the problem. His growing interest in the mystical — castles and so forth — plus his total belief in the pre-eminence of lead guitar, conspired to make our relationship increasingly difficult."

Also, Ian Gillan quoted what Roger Glover made of the Gillan/Blackmore friction during the making of *Fireball*. Fair play to Gillan for quoting Glover on the matter, I think that's good in the interest of balance and perspective as in, it is a second opinion rather than Gillan outright having a moan about Blackmore.

As Roger described things; "During *Fireball*, Ian seemed to go off the rails, with attitude and drinking problems. I've searched my memory to try and work out why he went down that route. He and Ritchie were at complete loggerheads and Ian may have got to the point where he thought 'I'm the singer of the band — if Ritchie can behave like that, so can I' so he became just as big an arsehole. It might have been the night Ritchie came into the studio after Ian had just done a vocal and said to him, 'that's shit' and walked out. So Ian started to fly everywhere in his own plane, stay in a separate hotel, take his own driver — Ossie Hoppe — who's now one of the biggest promoters in the business, based in Germany."

Sometimes it is hard to ascertain where the line may have sat between healthy competition and the not so healthy kind. Ian Gillan was quoted in March 1976 in *Sounds*; "Ritchie said to me, one day at the end of a series of rehearsals before Purple started going on tour, he came up to me and said 'if you start putting on a good show, really doing well then I'm going to try and blow you out. That'll make you do better and it'll make me do better' so me and Ritchie had a great threatening hold on Purple, the music never suffered. There was a great sense of competition between us."

Conflict between Gillan and Blackmore — whether petty squabbles or even full-blown arguments — weren't good for morale. Also, health problems seemed to be pretty universal for most members of the band at times. Jon Lord would often be suffering with back pain as a result of an injury that he got from carrying his kit in and out of clubs in the days of his previous band before Deep Purple, The Artwoods. Also, Roger Glover was struggling with stomach problems where, at the time, the cause was unknown.

Even though Glover's pain was eventually chalked up as being down to stress that could be resolved with meditation, it can't have been pleasant at the time and the unknown nature of it probably didn't help either. On top of that, the gruelling tour schedule in and of itself must have been exhausting and then, on top of that, the limited opportunity to have a break from each other's company must have surely exacerbated tensions and stress, both for the individuals and for the band as a unit. Oh, and of course, there was the pressure to follow up *In Rock* with an album that was just as good, if not better. That is a lot on the plate of a band who, in context, were still very much at the start of their careers; there was still so much to prove and so much to do in circumstances that were certainly less than stable and comfortable.

Immediately after the release of *In Rock*, Deep Purple toured for fifteen months straight. The touring began in July 1970 and ran until September 1971. Deep Purple visited three continents; Europe, North America and Australia. *Fireball* was initially intended for release by late 1970 but it didn't see its first release until July 1971, which was in the US. So much time was spent on the road that when a small window

The Making Of Fireball

in which to relax became available, it was often spent in the pub and apparently, in particular, Ian Gillan had begun to drink a lot more.

Jon Lord also had a lot on his plate. His wife had recently given birth to their daughter Sara and he needed to drive them back to London when the child got ill. This resulted in him missing three days worth of recording sessions. It turned into a large-scale argument that saw Lord threatening to leave the band entirely.

In an interview with Jerry Bloom for *More Black Than Purple* in 2007, Lord explained that despite rumours that he'd threatened to quit in 1969 as a result of the concerto, it was during the making of *Fireball* where things really got heated: "We were down in Devon and my wife had just had a baby and I drove back in the middle of some writing sessions overnight, before the M5 existed, horrendous journey and picked up my wife and baby then drove them right back down again. Back into writing sessions, twenty-four to thirty-six hours later, my new baby got a terrible cold because this place we were in was damp and awful and my wife just threw a wobbler and said I've got to go back to London so I drove her back again and then drove back down again, thus missing two or three days of the writing sessions. They were not happy about that and rightly so, although perhaps they could have been a bit kinder given the circumstances. So a big argument blew up about that and I threatened to quit for some strange reason but of course it was just one of those moments: 'oh fuck it I'm going to leave' and walked out and slammed the door."

"It was nothing to do with the concerto. Those things have been conflated and put together as a single happening whereas it was not. I mean they did find it difficult dealing with the orchestra during the concerto but watch the video and look at the smiles on their faces at the end of it all. One might say some of those smiles might be smiles of relief but they knew that we'd had a success. They knew that something grand had happened and it was only trying to take it further where the schism became apparent. I never pushed it. I didn't want to go round the world with orchestras. I was very happy to be a rock 'n' roll musician inside Deep Purple. I loved it and I think my playing in the band over the years makes that self-evident."

"A lot of rock 'n' roll "history" is by its own nature based on the comments that people make to journalists. Especially in the young part of the band before people have written their autobiographies. Sometimes people say things in anger or in exasperation or in fun and it becomes kind of the bible, when in actual fact when you look back and sort it out it isn't quite as black and white as that. I mean Ritchie might have said one day in 1970 'oh that fucking concerto, I could have done without that' whereas the night after we did it, he was: 'what a fabulous experience', he really enjoyed playing it. So you don't necessarily have to take it with a pinch of salt but you have to kind of sort it out into what was actually meant and what wasn't. Then you have to sort out the things that have become the myths that have grown up and become the accepted story. I haven't a problem with that, I don't go around waving a flag about it but when somebody such as yourself asks me I'm quite happy to set what I believe the record to be, straight."

Around the time of working on *Fireball*, Ritchie Blackmore had to have his appendix removed. It was hoped initially that the album would be recorded as quickly as *In Rock* had been but, with so much going on, it didn't work out that way.

As was reported in *Record Mirror* in October 1970, "Though work has started on the band's sixth album, it is unlikely to be on sale before Christmas due to touring pressures." And then, in March 1971, Ian Gillan was quoted in *New Musical Express* as he revealed; "The next album would have been ready by now but we had to hold it back a bit because of Ritchie's operation. It should be ready for the mixing stage and the artwork by mid-April. Five tracks are done and there will be seven or eight included."

Roger Glover was quoted in *The Quietus* in January 2011 as he explained that by the time of *Fireball*, it was only him and Ian Paice who were reliably present for the mixing sessions; "It was just me and Ian Paice but I don't think it's because the others didn't think it was important. By that time, any studio album we made, no one showed up for except me and Paice. When we made *Deep Purple In Rock* all five were there, interested. By *Fireball* people were sort of like, 'I've had enough now, I'm going home' and by *Machine Head*, it was again just me and Paice. But it wasn't because we thought the album was going to turn out bad."

As seasoned as all members of Deep Purple MkII were as

musicians by the time things had started to take off for them commercially, the large scale on which it happened after the release of *In Rock* was such that it is absolutely plausible that there could have been a real sense of being overwhelmed. As individuals, they had worked hard to get there.

As *Melody Maker* reported in October 1970; "Now it's Purplemania. Deep Purple are the latest group to attract Beatlemania scenes in the north of England." Roger Glover told *New Musical Express* in June 1971; "Before I joined the band I was studying interior design but I didn't really enjoy it and I became a very unsuccessful musician for a very long time. It's only been the last few years that's turned me on. I've never regretted anything I've done, you only really look back on the good times. I think any faith Deep Purple had in me was blind faith and I'm very grateful to them for what they've done for me."

Talk about going from one extreme to the other! That could have been a factor that informed some of the pressure that the band felt when it came to making *Fireball*. In Ian Gillan's autobiography, he described how during the making of *Fireball*, the tour schedule had begun to feel more hectic due to the success of *In Rock* and also, there were days where he missed the normal day to day life of not being a rock star. He described with candour some elements of the superficial nature of the whole thing; "We needed to straighten people out about who we were and we did this through a period of heavy touring, rock 'n' roll behaviour and the release of our album, *Deep Purple In Rock* in June 1970."

The sessions for the album that would come to be known as *Fireball* began in September 1970 but Deep Purple's touring schedule resulted in the process being very much one of a start-stop affair; there was little scope for continuity. By December 1970, the band, along with family and roadies, went to The Hermitage farmhouse in Welcombe, Devon.

In all fairness, quite a lot was achieved during this time whereby the following songs were written; 'Strange Kind Of Woman', 'Freedom', 'Slow Train' and 'The Mule'. 'Grabsplatter', an older instrumental, was also reworked into the track, 'I'm Alone'. Roger Glover used a Revox tape recorder to capture the jam sessions that resulted in 'Strange Kind Of Woman' being written. He had purchased

Deep Purple - Fireball: In-depth

the tape recorder when he first had some disposable income and had brought it with him to use for the first time at the The Hermitage. The working title for 'Strange Kind Of Woman' was 'Prostitute' and 'Freedom' started out as 'Born To Live'. It was in London in the January and February of 1971 that more progress was made.

There were four Scottish tour dates that had originally been scheduled for the end of January 1971 but they were rescheduled for early March to allow for more time in the studio to work on *Fireball*. On the 25th Anniversary edition of *Fireball* released in 1996, Roger Glover wrote for the liner notes; "The eight-track recording with Martin Birch engineering was at the studio in which we'd finished *In Rock*, De Lane Lea in Kingsway. That we felt comfortable in this basement studio is obvious as we recorded the majority of the tracks there — 'Fireball', 'Demon's Eye', 'Fools', 'No No No', 'Strange Kind Of Woman', 'Anyone's Daughter' and 'No One Came'." The first track to be recorded was 'Anyone's Daughter' and 'Strange Kind Of Woman' was also one of the earliest to be recorded of all the songs for *Fireball*. On top of this disjointed method of working, Deep Purple were then approached by Harvest to provide a single for pre-release; something that would get people interested prior to the release of the actual *Fireball* album. The song chosen to fulfil this duty was 'Strange Kind Of Woman' and this is why this particular song wasn't included on the UK version of *Fireball*. As a single, 'Strange Kind Of Woman' did well. It entered the chart at number twenty-nine in March; not bad going at all considering that there was a nationwide postal strike at the time which resulted in compromised scope for record retailers.

The 'Strange Kind Of Woman' single was reviewed in *New Musical Express* as they tipped it for chart success in February 1971; "Deep Purple Do Themselves Really Proud…It says much for Deep Purple that, despite the large number of groups currently churning out heavy music, it has still managed to develop a distinctive sound of its own. This latest single again generates the outfit's own particular brand of hard rock — yet, for all the earthiness and thickness, its noteworthy for the tight performance and quality of musicianship. The beat is penetrating and compelling, the vocal is spirited and gutsy, and the guitars are pungent and reverberating. The melody line

The Making Of Fireball

is little more than a repetitive riff — which let's face it, it the basis of all pure rock. Midway through the set, there's an unexpected slow passage of considerable delicacy that's effective because of its sharp contrast from the remainder of the routine. Another good one from Purple, which should do the lads proud."

The single was reviewed in *Record Mirror* the same month; "Not the best of the Purple patches, not by a long chalk, but there's a lot of earnest endeavour on this sometimes stilted offering. Given a couple of plays, it takes on greater depth though — and it's definitely a good, tight, punchy sound. Nice rotating figures and it's obviously a chart cert."

By late March 1971, 'Strange Kind Of Woman' was sitting at a comfortable number eight in the British top ten charts alongside some classic and well known songs; 'Rose Garden' by Lynn Anderson, 'My Sweet Lord' by George Harrison, 'Sweet Caroline' by Neil Diamond and 'Pushbike Song' by The Mixtures. 'Hot Love' by T-Rex was at number one during that week. Ian Gillan said of the single; "As with most progressive hard rock bands for that period, we avoided singles but 'Strange Kind Of Woman' ('I'm Alone' on the B-side) was released in February, and the album was on the shelves in time for our second American tour."

In a relatively recent interview, Jon Lord (easily post 2000) said of 'Strange Kind Of Woman'; "'Strange Kind Of Woman' was again, not done as part of the album sessions, I don't think. I seem to remember the same kind of pressure for a single was put on us and 'Strange Kind Of Woman' was an attempt, really, to cash in — if you like — on the success of 'Black Night', it uses the same shuffle tempo. I think it's a very successful song because it was also a big hit, but it produced a really good on stage song — so did 'Black Night' incidentally, still to this day — but most of the *Fireball* stuff was written on the north Cornwall coast down at a place called Welcombe Bay — a really spooky old semi derelict house, we seemed to have a penchant for semi derelict spooky houses a long way from anywhere. I think that house has recently been back on the market, and in the publicity material for the sale of the house was, I think it said it was Deep Purple's recording studio, which was rather stretching the truth."

Just to clarify, Welcombe Bay is actually in Devon but right on

Deep Purple - Fireball: In-depth

the border with Cornwall, hence it is often referred to as being in the more southern of the two counties. But talk of 'Strange Kind Of Woman' involves a contentious issue raised by Ritchie Blackmore's recollections in his 1995 interview with Neil Jeffries: "We were told to go back and write a single (January 1971), so we booked some studio time and arranged to meet. When I got there we were all there but Jon. I phoned the office and said: 'Look, the four of us are here and ready but there's no sign of Jon'. 'Oh, he's here', they said. 'What's he doing in London, he should be here to write and record? Put him on'. 'I, err, I had some things to do. Carry on without me, you don't need me to be there.' So we did. We sat around and came up with 'Strange Kind Of Woman', and after we'd recorded it I remember Paicey coming over to me and saying: 'You don't think Jon is going to expect his name on the writing credits for that, is he?' And I said: 'I'll bet he does, why not ask him?' Sure enough, he did — he insisted on it! I couldn't really take him seriously after that."

The UK leg of Deep Purple's tour was due to finish in Aberdeen on the 8th March. It was on that date that Roger Glover collapsed on stage, reaching an agonising climax as a result of the stomach pains he'd had for a while during that tour. The signs that he was not well had certainly been there in the run up to this occurrence; There had been occasions where Chas Hodges (from support band Heads, Hands & Feet) had, had to stand in for him by the time shows got to the encore stage. Ritchie Blackmore was quoted in *Record Mirror* in May 1971, with his typically exaggerated dry sense of humour; "Our biggest problem is bass player Roger Glover, who is in a really bad way at the moment as every time he goes on stage he is in some considerable pain. He has tuberculosis of the liver and after each performance we have to stretch him out in the dressing room for an hour to recover. It looks almost certain that we will have to get a replacement for him on live gigs for a while."

Luckily, it turned out that it wasn't as serious as everyone had feared it to be at the time. Glover was quoted in February 1972 in *New Musical Express*; "Six months ago there were some rumours circulating around about me leaving the group because of illness. Every time we went on stage I had a bad pain where my appendix scar was. I spent a lot of money going to various doctors to find out what it was, but none of them could tell me. It got to the stage, in fact, where I was seriously thinking I'd have to leave the band because literally the pain was so bad I was doubled on stage. Anyway, my doctor suggested hypnosis, and after several treatments it worked, I've never had any trouble since."

Whilst it was very much to the relief of everyone concerned that ultimately, Glover's stomach pains were down to stress and nothing more sinister, it was not long after that Ritchie Blackmore was struck down with appendicitis As was reported in *New Musical Express* in March 1971; "Purple Extends Aussie Visit!... Deep Purple — which was to have made a whirlwind twenty-four hour visit to Australia for a one nighter and Sydney Randwick Stadium on May 9 — has now been asked to play three further concerts there. The group will now also appear at Perth Sebaeco Stadium (7), Melbourne Festival Hall (8) and Brisbane Festival Hall (10). Negotiations are also under way for Purple to play two concerts in Japan immediately after its Australian dates. Meanwhile, group member Ritchie Blackmore is now out of hospital after having his appendix removed and is convalescing at home. The rest of the outfit is holidaying until he is fit."

As was reported in *The Sydney Morning Herald* on 10th May 1971 under the headline, "30,000 Turn Up For Randwick Rock"; "The adrenalin pumping hard rock band, Deep Purple, pushed the crowd to its greatest fever. The versatile singer Ian Gillan is well known for his part as Christ in the rock opera, *Jesus Christ Superstar*. At the final ovation, the pale full moon rose and Deep Purple tinged the sky lilac. As the group finished, the members dashed off and airline trucks sped their equipment to catch flights to Melbourne, where an extra concert was scheduled last night." Bear in mind that where the reporter said that Deep Purple pushed the crowd it its greatest fever, the show had also included performances from Free and Manfred Mann.

Roger Glover told *New Musical Express* in June 1971; "We did two weeks in Germany, four dates in Italy and one in Zurich. While we were in Rome one of our roadies' father's died so we flew him home and that left one for the gear and one for us. After Italy we flew to Zurich but the big ends went on the lorry carrying the gear and the roadie was stuck in a village with very little money and not one solitary person spoke English. He phoned all the lorry rental

Deep Purple - Fireball: In-depth

firms but they put the phone down because he didn't speak Italian. He got through to the Zurich Hilton but couldn't reach us and we found out we didn't have the gear on the day of the concert. We tried every avenue of getting the gear there but everything was closed. Eventually we got the small amps and guitars on an executive jet and borrowed the rest to go on stage for seven thousand people. It was awful and we said, 'in future, no gear — no gig.' A week later, we did a gig in Luxembourg and the roadies got picked up in Italy where they were arrested for being suspected of causing an accident. There was a twelve-hour delay and they couldn't get to the gig in time so Deep Purple hired a plane for £1200 to fly the gear from Milan — that was just a personal expense. It was a good gig but talk about nervous breakdowns. We can give you a few. In Berlin, one of our roadies, Ron (Quinton), was changing a fuse and got an electric shock and nearly died, he was in a really bad state."

There certainly were challenges during the days of making *Fireball*. It's a difficult one because in many ways, such obstacles were not exclusive to *Fireball*. I mean, look at what happened with the famous flare gun incident in Montreux during the making of *Machine Head*. It is for this reason that I feel it is important to stipulate that it was probably not the case that making *Machine Head* was an absolute cakewalk in comparison to *Fireball*; the commercial success of *Machine Head* can all too easily be used to negate the challenges that Deep Purple may have had when making that album too.

That said, the illness that was going on with several members of the group during the days of making *Fireball* certainly had their elements of exception. In Ian Gillan's autobiography (the version released in 1998), he recalled; "There was no let-up in our touring schedule and 1971 saw us on a major UK tour where we pulled capacity crowds and were big box office. In February alone we did the Royal Albert Hall, Hull, Sheffield, Bournemouth, Portsmouth, Birmingham, Bristol, Plymouth, Manchester, Newcastle, Coventry, Leicester and Brighton. As such, our reputation precedes us, often to cause problems for all concerned... Our health should have alerted someone to question the routine."

Perhaps all the rigorous touring during the days that *Fireball* was being worked on was down to a feeling that it was necessary

The Making Of Fireball

to make the most of the public interest while it was there. Ritchie Blackmore said in *New Musical Express* in September 1971; "The trouble is, it's all got to be done. We've got to do it all to keep up with the people because they want it. Something comes along and you agree to it and you've forgotten about the first thing. We feel we owe the public something. If someone says 'can you do Vienna and Mannheim?' we think 'no, because we're rehearsing for the British tour' but we say yeah and do it. We prefer to be on stage and in the end you get more gigs than you want. To anyone, that's success... We were pressurised too much by the public in general. We don't get much time to write and that's a drag. In the end the public suffers because you don't have enough time to record and at the same time you can't always produce your best. We only had two months off to record. When you get to that stage, some aspects of your work have got to suffer. You do get a certain amount of enjoyment out of it. I enjoy tours for about a week but after that your equipment starts to break down and so do you yourself. You can't do it for more than seven nights running and I feel sorry for the person who comes on the eighth night. But you can't get together with the promoters and put anything off, you just have to go on and do it all until the end. It's a shame. It's disappointing, but someone has always got to miss out, you can't play your best every night."

Ian Gillan said in August 1970 in *Melody Maker*; "If Frank Sinatra, the Beatles or Dylan were continually on the road, they would have died years ago. Not that I'm comparing us to them, although maybe we are as good. But it's very easy to become over exposed. A year ago we decided to concentrate mostly on this country (UK) and the continent."

In the same interview, Ritchie Blackmore was quoted; "We feel that we have accomplished what we set out to do. So now I think it's time we cut down in this country (UK) and concentrated on other countries a bit more."

Further sessions for *Fireball* took place in May before Deep Purple were due for their first shows in Australia. It was US audiences who would get the first taste of *Fireball* as it was released there in July; Warner Bros. had stipulated the necessity of this because they wanted the release of *Fireball* to coincide with Deep Purple's American tour dates.

Deep Purple - Fireball: In-depth

The American response towards *Fireball* was pretty decent. On 21st August, *Fireball* entered the *Billboard* chart in America and within a matter of just weeks, it was close to being in the top thirty. It was the fastest extent of travel up the American chart since the MkI album, *Shades Of Deep Purple*. *Fireball* was reviewed in *Cash Box* in August 1971; "How much longer will it be before Deep Purple gets the acceptance in America which they deserve? Although they have half a dozen LPs in release here and despite the devotion of the fans they have collected, they have yet to attain the popularity level they enjoy in England and elsewhere. *Fireball* should change that. It's an important new album. On it, the quintet deftly carve out seven crystal clear rock works, of which, 'Strange Kind Of Woman' and 'Anyone's Daughter' loom as most formidable. How much longer?!"

The 'Fireball' single was reviewed in *Cashbox* in October 1971; "It took a while but Deep Purple have finally succeeded in gaining the acceptance they so rightfully deserve. Now comes the title track of their most recent album effort guaranteed to expose the British rockers to the waiting AM audiences."

Once in America, Deep Purple joined up to tour with the Faces, who had already been gigging there for a while by that point. Ritchie Blackmore was quoted in September 1971 in *New Musical Express*; "The Faces pulled the crowd and we appealed to the Faces' crowd. We were prepared to be second to the Faces but in certain places people would say 'why are you second to the Faces?' They are very big in America. It was a very, very good tour — both for us and the tour as a whole. We'd have to do very, very well but at the same time they'd have to pull their fingers out to follow us."

Their music styles were very different but they seemed to share common ground when it came to throwing a good after party. The infamous evening of Rod Stewart inviting the entire audience back to Deep Purple's hotel happened during this tour. The result was a bill for $25,000, sent to Warner Bros., due to the damage done to the hotel from a food fight started by Ritchie Blackmore and Rod Stewart. Too bad camera phones didn't exist then! I bet something like that would have got a lot of YouTube views today. Ian Gillan recalled; "About three thousand kids turned up in the lobby. It became one long session of chaos, a beach party where all the straw shades were torched and a bash upstairs where Rod and Ritchie started throwing food at everyone, and when Russ Shaw from Warner Brothers tried to intervene later, they dumped him in a bath. The hotel manager came to complain and Ritchie bundled him up with a fire hose, at which point I decided to moon naked with a newspaper on fire, wedged up my bum. Sadly, the police spoilt our fun, which cost the record company about $25,000."

Still, at least it was perhaps a bit of light relief from the rigours of the intense touring schedule. Ritchie Blackmore told *Record Mirror* in May 1971; "America is obviously of paramount importance to us and this will be our chance to build upon the success of *In Rock*. Personal promotion is a must over there and we are going out with the Faces who are breaking big out there so it should help us. Personally I'm not looking forward to the travelling because we are already working ourselves into an early grave, but naturally I wouldn't consider ducking out for those reasons although it's possible we may find a deputy for me on the Australian tour."

For a gig at Long Beach that Deep Purple played with the Faces, (recorded by a local radio station and released in 2015) the hectic nature of life on the road was well documented by journalist, Allan McDougall in *Sounds* in August 1971. He quoted Jon Lord as having said upon their meeting up for the interview; "I came in early to buy an organ — bloody airlines dropped mine." Annoying but an occupational hazard I suppose. In the same interview, Lord continued; "Actually, it's been the best tour Deep Purple have done of the States. The most worthwhile so far. Gigging with the Faces has been so good. You know, obviously in most places we've played it's been their audiences — Especially in Detroit and Chicago, which is where Rod Stewart's label, Mercury, is headquartered. But in Texas, it seemed like they'd all come to see Deep Purple. Anyway, we usually had to work very hard to get the audiences going, and always got encores — which meant that the Faces also had to work especially hard to follow us. All of which meant a lot of fun for the audiences at every show... Did you know that our new album, *Fireball*, shipped 55,000 in the last three days? At last Deep Purple are going to really do it in the States, and there's re-orders coming into Warner's from all over the place."

Deep Purple - Fireball: In-depth

Busy times indeed! Deep Purple travelled home to the UK in late July where they found themselves with six weeks off prior to Harvest releasing *Fireball* in the UK. As Ian Gillan put it; "Frank Zappa once said that a musician can go crazy on tour — the hotel life, concerts and aeroplanes. I think perhaps the American trip with the Faces pushed us that way, and it was important to go back to the UK to rediscover our perspective and sanity."

It was more of a break for some than others though. Lord, Glover and Paice began working on the studio recording of *Gemini Suite* prior to regrouping in September for the British leg of tour.

By this time, they were already writing material for *Machine Head*; 'Highway Star', followed by 'Lazy'. Meanwhile, sales of *Fireball* in the UK were shooting upwards, and rapidly so. It got to number one but here's the kicker; it didn't stay there for long and overall, the sales of it just weren't comparable to *In Rock*. Equally, the single, 'Fireball' sold a tiny amount compared to sales of the band's earlier single, 'Black Night'.

Ritchie Blackmore said in *Sounds* in February 1974; "*Fireball*, we had no time to make whatsoever and although we've got very good management, I blame them for that because they expected us to tour the whole world and make an album at the same time. I was very angry at the time because I thought how do they expect us to make an album. We went into the studio knocking out secondary riffs and padding all the way through all the time and the whole LP to me was a failure except a few things."

By December, Deep Purple were in Switzerland working on *Machine Head*. With 'Fireball' having been released as a single on 29th October, it appeared on 2nd December 1971 on *Top Of The Pops* albeit it with Pans People dancing to the song. However, the band flew back to the UK to record and perform the song in the BBC studios on 15th December, with the performance broadcasted the following evening on *Top Of The Pops*.

It was back to Switzerland the next day to continue making the new album and it was effectively the end for the songs from *Fireball* as the band was more enamoured with the new material and by the time the band went back on the road in 1972 the set was largely built around *Machine Head*.

Cassette sleeve

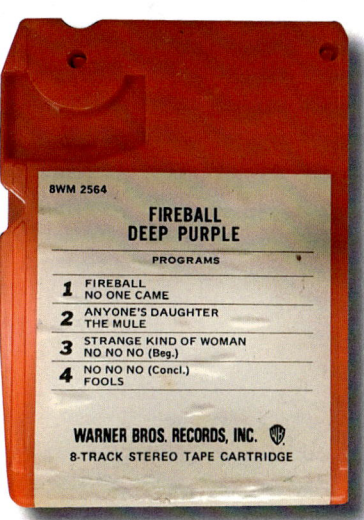

US 8 track

Fireball was released by Warners in North America and Japan two months before EMI released it throughout Europe and elsewhere. 'Strange Kind Of Woman' had to be included on this initial release as the band hadn't finished the final song for the album but Warners were adamant that the album should be available to coincide with the American tour.

Artists would put a lot of thought into an album's running order but the tape formats often necessitated changes so that the sides were even in length. But merely switching sides one and two on the cassette seemed bizarre.

Japanese first press

Japanese promo sleeve

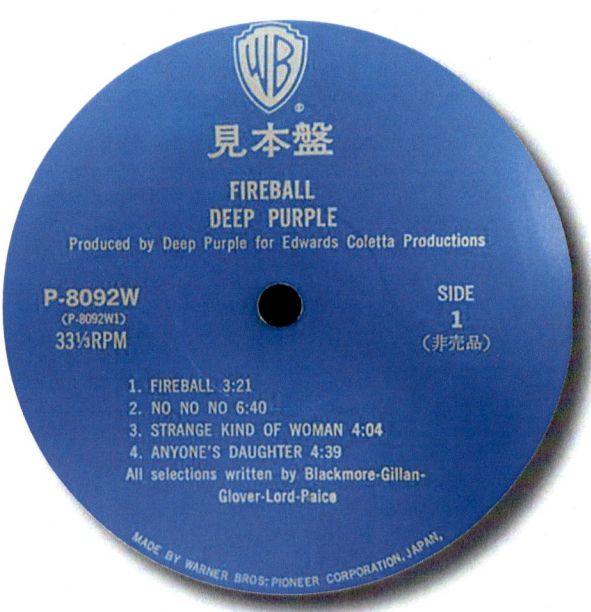

The Japanese release came with the usual obi strip that would list the song titles and other information in Japanese. The original release was, like the US version on the olive green Warners label, but the promotional copies had blue labels, as well as a more elaborate obi strip.

UK first press

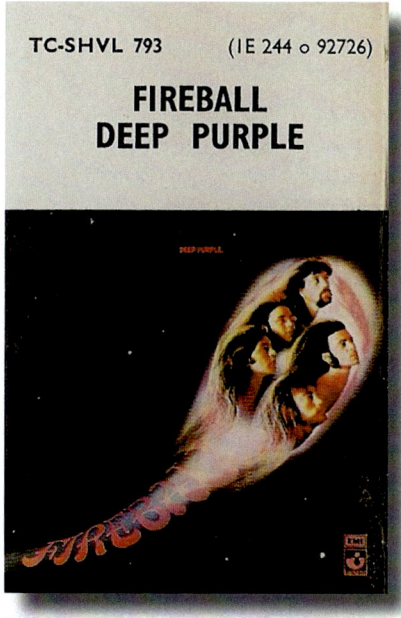

UK cassette

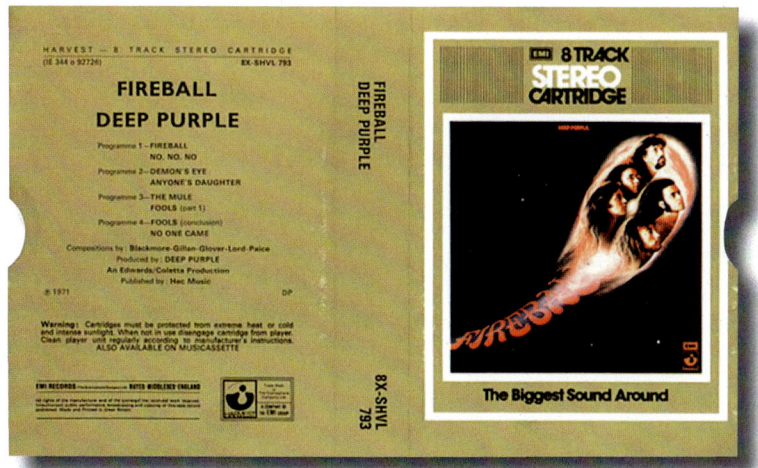

UK 8 track

There were some unusual variations of the album sleeve. After the initial Warners release in July, the rest of the world had the album in September, albeit with 'Demon's Eye' replacing 'Strange Kind Of Woman'.

The initial vinyl releases, like in the States and Japan, came with a two-sided lyric sheet. Whereas the Warners one was black and white, EMI's was a differently designed one and purple and white.

Early vinyl pressings are identified with "The Gramophone Co. Ltd" on the text going around the top of the label. By early 1974 that wording had changed to "EMI Records Ltd".

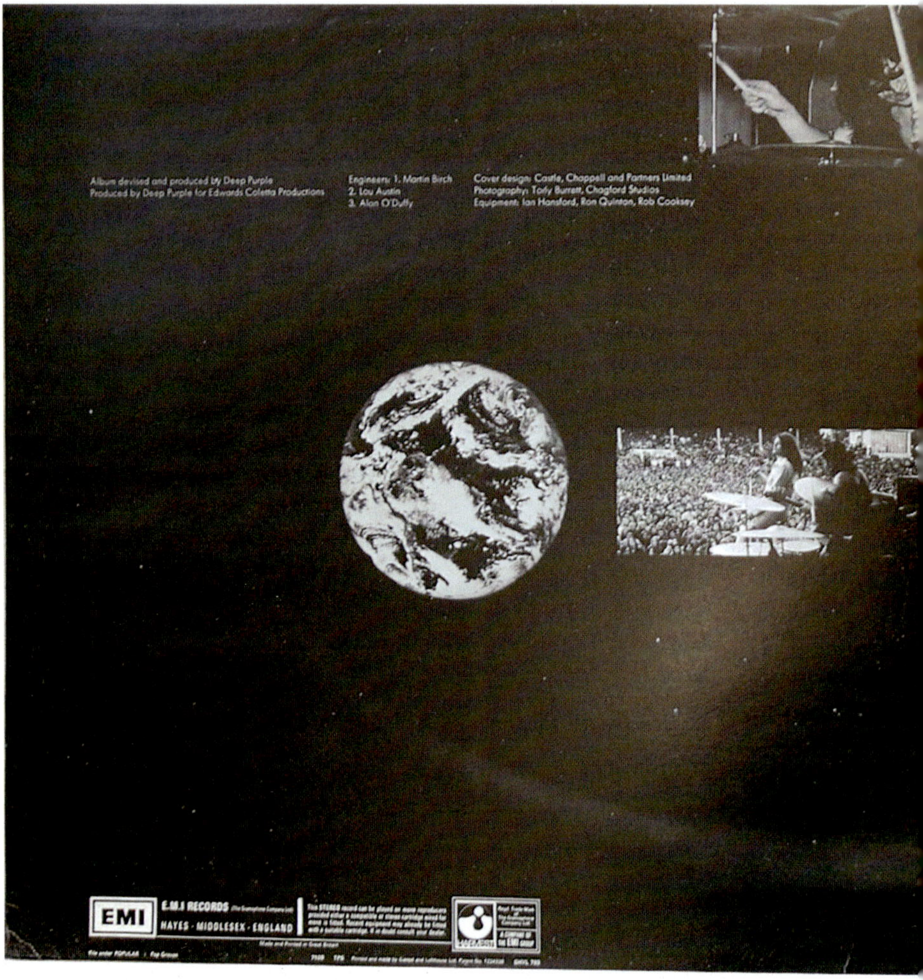

Venezuela back cover

Israel back cover

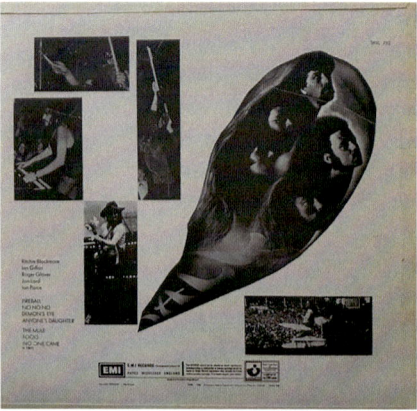

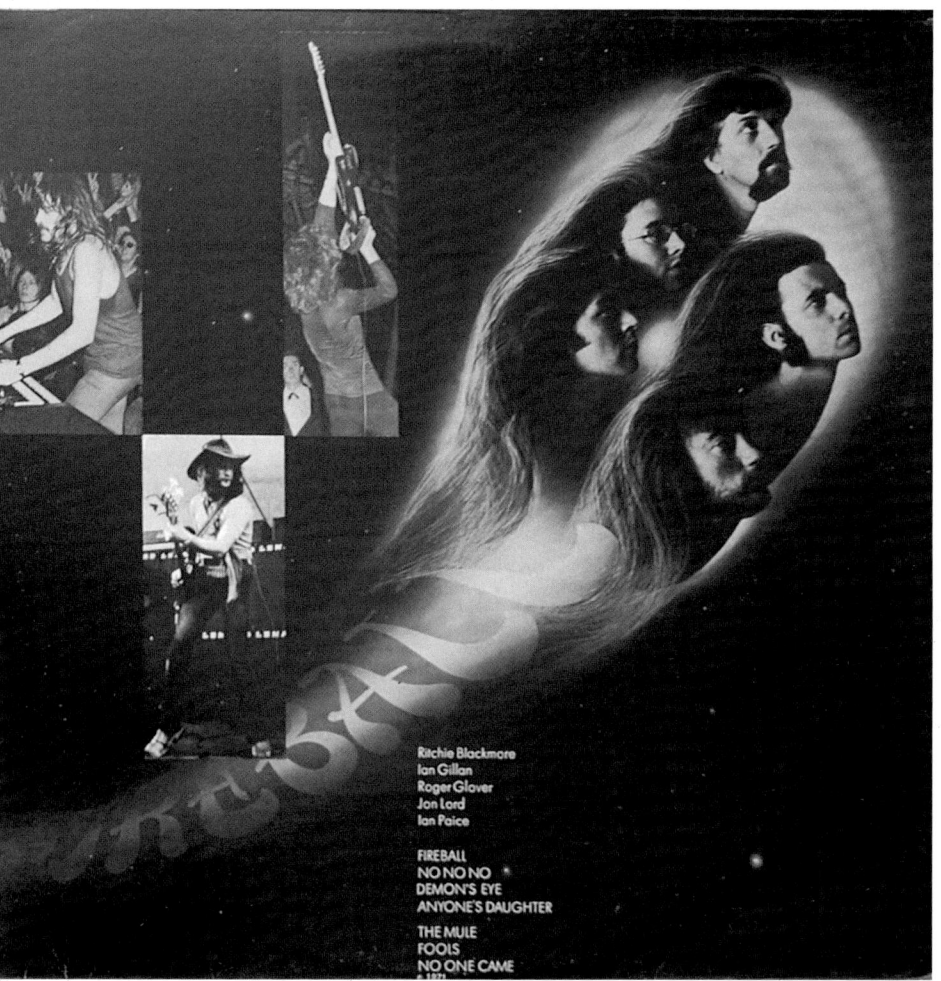

The album was initially released in a gatefold sleeve. The inside spread was monochrome and included a live photo of the band on stage at the Randwick Stadium, in Australia from the tour in May '71. Some countries released the album in a single sleeve and used parts of the inner spread design for the back sleeve. This certainly threw up some oddities as these versions from Israel and Venezuela show. Apparently the chap on the back of the Venezuelan cover was a very high-profile disc jockey in that country!

Israel

Philippines

Portugal

Brazil

Even though the album was released on Harvest in Israel, the label design was completely different. Elsewhere, the album was licensed to different labels around the world as these examples show.

Deep Purple - Fireball: In-depth

and will have its first two record set released November 1. Deep Purple are enjoying their greatest US success with *Fireball*."

Predominantly, I would argue at least, that ye olde internet is full of so much bull dink on the information front when it comes to stating when *Fireball* was actually released. To be fair, it's quite a complicated one because there are multiple factors at play here. Firstly, it is definitely the case that different parts of the world had significantly different albums released under the name of *Fireball* (significant insofar as, either including 'Demon's Eye' or 'Strange Kind Of Woman').

The UK version of *Fireball* had 'Demon's Eye' as the third track and 'Strange Kind Of Woman' was released as a single there. It was vice versa for the US, Canadian and Japanese releases of the album.

In the UK, the 'Strange Kind Of Woman' single got to number eight and the album's title track was also released as a single which got to number fifteen. Now then, regional variations were not a new and exclusive thing for Deep Purple album releases. Even with *In Rock*, the extended organ solo at the start of the opening track, 'Speed King' was in place on the UK release of the album but this wasn't the case on other regions in which the album was released.

It's mind blowing to think that in the days before Amazon and YouTube, it was most likely the case that people predominantly only had access to the version of an album that was released for the region in which they lived. To think that only in the UK did people get easy access to the phenomenal beginning of 'Speed King' on *In Rock*; Jon Lord's organ solo is a vital ingredient regarding the anticipation it creates prior to Blackmore's intense guitar chord opening to the song. It's a bit of a yin yang thing I suppose in how the two complement each other. Having purchased the Japanese version of the band score for *In Rock* a good few years ago now, I was disappointed that the sheet music for Lord's organ solo at the beginning of 'Speed King' wasn't there but then of course why would it be when the sheet music was reflective of the version of the song that Japanese listener's would probably be most familiar with? For what it's worth, I purchase the Japanese version of band scores simply because they are easier to get hold of generally speaking. It's an official product and all that good stuff, it's just made for the Japanese market.

Chapter Four
Strange Kind Of Release Dates

The release of *Fireball* in the States by Warner Bros. was part of a massive campaign to promote British artists. As well as the looming US tour dates, this was a factor in the urgency to get *Fireball* released in the US. As was reported in *Cashbox* in October 1971; "Warner Bros. records is launching a major merchandising promo, advertising and publicity campaign on behalf of twelve of its British acts who will be touring the North American continent this fall. Under the banner "The British Invasion Fall '71", the programme features specially created displays, posters, press kits, and a full line of stationary supplies. Print and radio advertising have been specifically devised to saturate national and local markets with data concerning each group's personal appearances and albums. The Warner Bros./Reprise roster of British talent, the label noted, accounts for a considerable amount of the company's sales. During October and November, US and Canadian concert halls will be taken over by Black Sabbath, Jethro Tull, Faces, Kinks, Deep Purple, Fleetwood Mac, Pentangle, T Rex, Colosseum, Curved Air, Quiver and Daddy Cool. To fully exploit each group's individual popularity, Warner Bros. has coincided the "English Invasion" with the release of albums from the members of the label's English family. Radio spots in major markets across the country have been purchased by Warner Bros. to support the group's albums, as well as a special merchandising project that will focus on each group's entire Warner Bros./Reprise catalogue. Black Sabbath, Jethro Tull, and Deep Purple are all currently riding high on the charts. Black Sabbath's third album, *Masters Of Reality*, earned the quartet its third consecutive gold album and has already sold more than 600,000 LPs. Jethro Tull is currently represented on the charts with its Gold album, *Aqualung*,

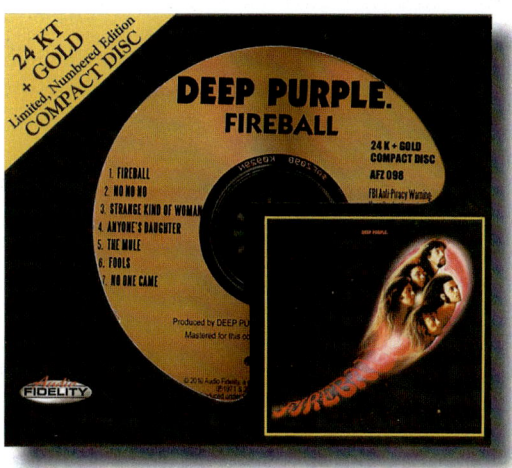

In 2010 Steve Hoffman remastered the MKII catalogue for limited edition releases in the States on CDs plated with 24 karat gold. Only the original master mixes were used and played back on a specially constructed vintage playback deck. Each analogue master was put through a proprietary analogue to digital converter which reinforced the resolution of the original masters without any further sonic manipulation. Each master was shipped directly to the manufacturing plant for etching in real time onto the glass surface by laser.

2018 purple vinyl.   2019 purple vinyl.

The resurgence in popularity of vinyl has seen the album reissued in that format several times in recent years. Both the 2016 180gram and 2019 purple vinyl US releases actually were of the European version of the album with 'Demon's Eye'. It was also released on purple vinyl in 2018 in the UK.

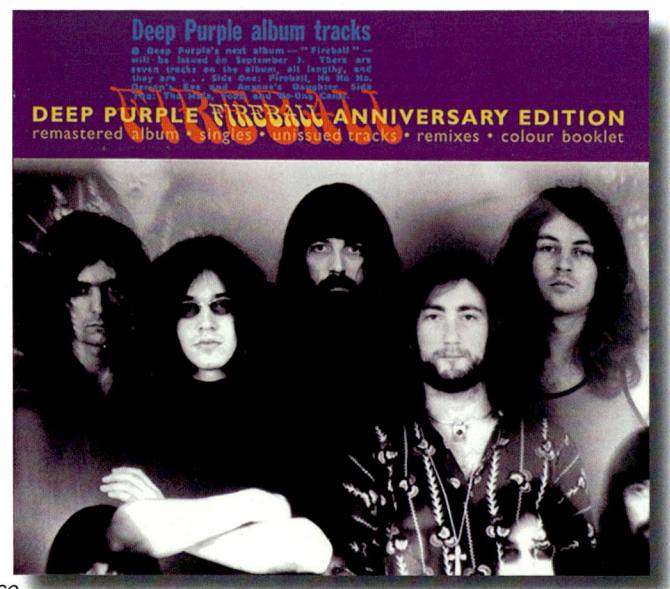

UK slip case

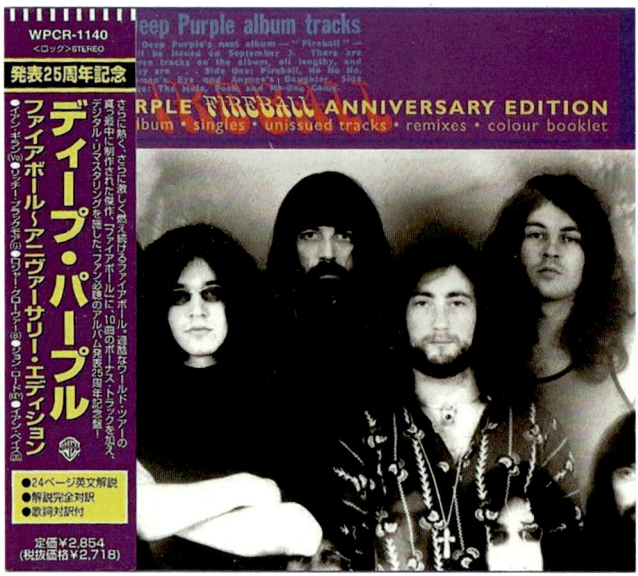

Japanese slip case

In 1996 the 25th anniversary of the album was commemorated with Roger Glover remixing it as well as adding some additional material from the sessions. The CD was released in a slipcase. There was also a limited edition double vinyl version.

Even though the Japanese version included the usual obi, it wasn't actually released there until the following year. Even more bizarrely, the anniversary edition CD wasn't released in the States until 2000!

Strange Kind Of Release Dates

So yes, regional differences were not a new thing when it came to *Fireball* (and again, such differences are reflected in the Japanese band score book that I managed to get hold of for *Fireball*; there is a band score for 'Strange Kind Of Woman' but not for 'Demon's Eye' because the content of the sheet music is reflective of the album released in Japan). The point I'm making is this; with the differences in album content being regionally different, it does make sense that *Fireball* did not have a universal release date.

There are so many possible reasons for the regional variations in terms of content but the real reason is revealed further on in the story.

As was reported in *Cashbox* in February 1972; "(In Germany) Deep Purple are more successful at present than the Beatles. The album, *Deep Purple In Rock* reached higher sales than the Beatles album, *Sergeant Pepper*. Their new album, *Fireball*, has sold 100,000 copies to date."

As was reported in *Record World* in March 1972; "Comin' up on the national (German) charts is *Fireball* by Deep Purple, released by Wilfred Jung on Electrola, backed by FD and H's team from Hamburg."

There just seems to have been so many scheduling problems when it came to *Fireball* and this was probably to the band's embarrassment at times. It really comes across that when it came to marketing *Fireball* and indeed Deep Purple at the time, many things were quite wonky. Take what happened in Germany with the Gold discs that had to be cut in half for instance. As was reported in *Cashbox* in April 1972; "Deep Purple, who have become the most popular foreign rock group in Germany, have received an award for their new album, *Fireball*. Their German recording company, EMI/Electrola, Cologne, presented them with "half" a Golden Record. Deep Purple were awarded a trophy for this record during a press conference which appropriately took place in front of a furnace in a large German steel refinery."

In the photograph for the report, everyone is wearing safety hats. In the 1991 Paul Justman directed documentary, *Deep Purple: Heavy Metal Pioneers*, Roger Glover said; "Deep Purple *In Rock* went huge and it stayed in the charts for a year and we toured in the wake of that pretty extensively around Europe. It didn't happen in America.

Deep Purple - Fireball: In-depth

So we'd kind of forgotten America for a while and concentrated on Europe. And then we did the follow up album, *Fireball*. As an album it didn't do anything like what *Deep Purple In Rock* had done. In fact, I remember going to Germany once and they had expected it to be Gold by the time we got there and it wasn't, but they had all the presentation and the party all lined-up, so they decided to go ahead with that anyway and presented us with half a Gold Record. They'd actually cut down the middle and we didn't know whether to laugh or whether to be insulted and walk away."

There certainly seemed to be a culture surrounding *Fireball* of "it's not *In Rock!*" *Fireball* was reviewed in *Sounds* in September 1971; "Purple's place in British rock music is assured, which is just as well because there isn't too much on *Fireball* that would further their cause, apart from two good tracks 'Demon's Eye' and 'Fools'. The feel of the album, apart from these two numbers, is dominated by the drums/bass/guitar heaviness that is almost impossible to escape from with bands in Deep Purple's musical area. True, 'Anyone's Daughter' is a chirpy little ditty with acoustic guitar and piano, but unfortunately it doesn't work. 'Fireball', the opening track, bursts out from the speakers like a bomb, a breakneck number urged on by Ian Paice's drums, stabbing guitar and some space-age Lord organ, by comparison 'No No No' is quite leisurely, but 'Demon's Eye' rocks better than any of its predecessors. Ian Gillan bares his chest more, Jon Lord lays down some attractive organ parts and guitarist Ritchie Blackmore gets more of a chance to show his hand, the tranquillity and dream-like opening to 'Fools' — light organ lines and drums — is shattered by fine old heavy rock bass/drums throbbing and Gillan's rasping vocals. Add to this Blackmore's wah-wahing guitar and Gillan finally getting up a full head of steam and you have the only other good piece on the album. You can't help but get the feeling that Deep Purple could have come up with something better — there's no reason why all the tracks couldn't have been up to the standard of 'Demon's Eye' and 'Fools', the band are capable of it."

Now then, the actual release dates. There are some sources online that state that *Fireball* was released in the US in May 1971. I've looked into it as much as I possibly can and it was actually in July 1971. My reasoning behind this is that numerous sources state it as

Strange Kind Of Release Dates

being such and also, it was reported in *Record World* in August 1971; "WB (Warner Bros.) Announces Three Part Release... The Warner Reprise late summer album release will ship in three parts (a total of fifteen albums) and 'some of the most powerful musical products we've issued this year' according to Executive Vice President, Joe Smith. The first wave of three albums (shipped July 23rd) included *Paul And*, the first solo album by Paul Stookey, formerly of Peter, Paul And Mary. A single from this album, 'The Wedding Song (There Is Love)' is already charted on top forty stations across the country. Initial orders for *Paul And* indicate equal success. *Fireball* by Deep Purple is that English group's third for Warner Bros., released on the heels of their highly successful US tour. *The Mothers Live At The Fillmore* was the third in the release. Sales response for The Mothers (on Frank Zappa's Bizarre label, distributed by Reprise) indicates this might be the most successful Mothers album to date."

Notably, *Fireball* was Deep Purple's third album on Warner Bros. in the US because after *Shades Of Deep Purple*, *The Book Of Taliesyn*, *Deep Purple* and *Concerto For Group And Orchestra*, Tetragrammaton had gone bust and thus, Warner Bros. picked up, initially reissuing *Concerto For Group And Orchestra* in April 1970 and so had *In Rock* and *Fireball* too.

Across all of these albums, they were on release on Harvest (a division of EMI) in the UK with the exception of *Shades Of Deep Purple* which was released on Parlophone. The UK release date for *Fireball* is universally understood as being that of September 1971. As was reported in *New Musical Express* from the week ending 4th September 1971; "Purple will spend the whole of December recording a follow up album to *Fireball* which is released in Britain today (Friday 3rd) and the sessions are expected to take place in Switzerland using the Rolling Stones' mobile unit."

Deep Purple's first album, *Shades Of Deep Purple*, had been released in July 1968 in the US and September 1968 for the UK market. That comes across as a decision that probably made much sense at the time; although they were a British band, Deep Purple's following was very much an American one at that time in their career. It's plausible that engaging with the UK at the time was perhaps seen as a bit of a secondary necessity.

Deep Purple - Fireball: In-depth

But by the time of *Fireball* being released, Deep Purple were pretty much a known entity in both places as a result of the impact that *In Rock* had. Deep Purple had toured all over the place by then and prominently so. So why stagger the release dates of *Fireball* so significantly?

With the album recording sessions having stretched over several months, and with Warner Bros.' insistence that the album be released to coincide with the tour, the only option was to include 'Strange Kind Of Woman' as 'Demon's Eye' was not recorded until June and Warners' preparation for the album preceded that date.

Roger Glover was quoted in *New Musical Express* in June 1971; "The most important thing about the new one is to get it finished for America because we're going there in July. It's called *Fireball* and it will be out in July, or August at the latest. The British one will be better because we're putting 'Strange Kind Of Woman' on the American one and there'll be a completely new one on the British album."

In an interview that took place in early February 1971, Ian Gillan spoke with a sense of humour about the release dates of the 'Strange Kind Of Woman' single; "This next one is a new thing and it's actually being released as a single or something. I think it's either this Friday or next Friday, but I don't know which 'cos there's a lot of confusion over it. In fact it's a single and we recorded it just about two weeks ago and we wrote it in the same day just about half an hour after we recorded it! You'll have to excuse me, I'm confused about the whole thing."

Whichever regional release of *Fireball* is in question, the band overall still felt that it was a rushed job; recorded as a bit of a stressful afterthought and obligation that had to be completed swiftly whilst they were committed to that whacking great tour where Ian Gillan and then Ritchie Blackmore came down with hepatitis not long after.

As journalist, Steve Peacock, reported in *Sounds* in April 1972; "For the second time in six months, Deep Purple had to cut short an American tour, and both times for the same reason. Last time, Ian Gillan got ill with hepatitis, this time it was Ritchie Blackmore's turn." Jon Lord was quoted in the same feature; "I'm trying to work out what I've done wrong. It doesn't seem fair that the same group gets hit twice by hepatitis in six months — both times in the middle of an American tour. It seems that every time we go there we take two steps forward and one back."

Roger Glover said in June 1971 in *New Musical Express* as he explained the challenges of introducing new material from *Fireball* into the live set; "We tried playing a little bit of it at the Roundhouse at the Camden Festival. We tried doing 'Into The Fire' before 'In Rock' was released and it didn't go down that well. We did 'No One Came' at Camden and that didn't go down well either because it didn't have that magic, people weren't used to it. They wanted to hear old numbers. We have been criticised for not changing the stage act but people don't want us to change. It's a bit frustrating because you get very stale playing the same numbers. Another frustrating thing is you don't get time to rehearse, we haven't rehearsed since January — you come back from a tour and the last thing you want to do is rehearse."

It was certainly all happening! As the interviewer added, "Roger was feeling very tired when he arrived to meet me. He had been in the recording studio working on the last track of *Fireball* until six that morning and we had put our interview back by two and a half hours in order that he could get more sleep. At the best of times he isn't the fittest of people and he finds that the rigours of touring are taking their toll health-wise. He has been doing a good spot of producing lately, but there aren't many blank days on the date sheet."

Roger continued; "There isn't time to do anything else but play with Deep Purple, it's telling on all of us. It's getting to the stage, once we've broken America, of taking things easier. There's no point in killing yourself off, we could get to the stage where we could turn down work."

Deep Purple - Fireball: In-depth

Chapter Five

Bootlegging

Whilst the general feeling towards *Fireball* was perhaps a generally negative one at the time, at least from Deep Purple overall, the material from the album was used in the live sets, often providing something iconic. For instance, a fantastic drum solo from Ian Paice. As journalist, Richard Green, described the band's performance of 'The Mule' in September 1971 in *New Musical Express*; "Then we got 'The Mule', also from the album, and what Ian Gillan described as 'a perverted interpretation', little Ian got very busy taking his solo here instead of on 'Paint It, Black' and the feel of the number differed a lot from the one on record."

In the same feature, Roger Glover was quoted as he elaborated; "We rearranged it ('The Mule') and played a completely different rhythm from the record, which just didn't work on stage when we tried it a few months ago somewhere."

I would argue that this is what makes bootlegs of Deep Purple's live shows so vital. I think really it works on two levels as in firstly, many bootlegs stand as fantastic historic documentation of what the band sounded like at the time. Secondly, a lot of them just sound really good and for most fans who have listened to official releases over and over again, the bootlegs offer something different and for want of better term, new.

Deep Purple's reputation as a live band was arguably crucial to their success, even when it came to their breakthrough with *In Rock*. Roger Glover said in October 1972 in *New Musical Express*; "Before we had *In Rock* released, we spent six months going up and down the M1 playing maybe five gigs a week. We travelled all over England and were pulling in bigger audiences and getting better money than most of the chart bands. That was simply because our live show had

Deep Purple - Fireball: In-depth

a good reputation. Then when the album came out, that reputation made it sell, I'm sure of it. It got no radio play at all. The only thing that did was 'Black Night' and they only played that after it was a hit."

The reputation was certainly alive and well. The *Evening Post* reviewed a show that took place on 17th May 1970 in Bristol; "Deep Purple are noise. Loud, proud, mind-blasting noise. They exploit it, distort it, punish it. Their success or failure is measured in decibels. Ringed by towering banks of amplifiers they attack relentlessly. And if you don't like the result, you're not there anyway, because Deep Purple have a reputation for this kind of thing. Everyone knows what to expect and last night they got it. Two hours of screaming, nerve-wracking music that scored heavily for the band. They played tracks from the *Taliesyn* album — old rock numbers, now heavies. The haunting 'Child In Time' and a short drop in volume. But then it's back to the noise business — 'Speed King', 'Black Night', 'Mandrake Root'. Jon Lord wrenches impossible sounds from the organ. He also kicks it. The all-out effort ended with a grotesque mime to the flash-flash of strobe lighting, 'we're loud because we like to be', said the singer. They also have to be. It's a part of them and there's no going back now. Toned down it just wouldn't be the same. Ashton, Gardner and Dyke supported, with dominant organ producing disjointed sounds."

The success of *In Rock* was such that Deep Purple were in demand and with that, it wasn't long before bootlegs of their concerts were to follow. The infamous *H Bomb* bootleg appeared in late 1970. It was the subject of a court case that helped to make bootlegs illegal in Europe from early 1972. *H Bomb* features a live performance that took place in Aachen in early July 1970. It is a worthwhile listen because it documents the performance of a set list that features some pre *In Rock* numbers. Ian Gillan recalled; "Ritchie was capable of giving a great night out to the fans, as we developed a free flow set that took our music in various directions. It could always be said that no two Purple shows were ever the same, which is why bootlegging our music was such a great idea for certain entrepreneurs. Still — good luck to them, that's what I say. And, as the guitarist and I developed a close relationship on stage, the bond made for a dynamic show.

Bootlegging

With a great band behind us, impromptu moments were introduced. Ritchie would often mischievously go into riffs of 'Teddy Bear's Picnic' or 'In An English Country Garden'."

The gig that features on *H Bomb* wasn't that well documented at the time. That's fascinating when you consider that also on the bill were Free, Traffic, Pink Floyd and T-Rex. Jon Lord advocated that the bootleg was made as a result of someone cannily sneaking an eight-track mixer inside a Volkswagon and hid it under the stage. The band were actually quite impressed with the quality of the bootleg although of course, it wasn't without its controversy.

Roger Glover was quoted in June 1971 in *New Musical Express*, upon being shown a copy of *H Bomb* by the interviewer; "I view bootlegs with mild amusement. It's nice to be considered of the calibre where people will take the trouble to do it and I like to find out how much they make out of it and how it's turned out. I don't mind it that much."

But on the legal side of it, Glover added; "If you're going to be part of society you have to play by its rules, that's just not what's happening and the reason I'm against it. I bought a Deep Purple bootleg in Germany and it cost me a fiver, so they're making money out of me. You can stop the big operators because they have to have huge pressing plants and distributors and you can get an injunction, but you can't stop the small operators. I heard a Led Zeppelin bootleg that was so bad it cheered me up, I realised other groups have their off nights as well."

When Roger Glover was played a copy of *H Bomb* by the interviewer, he was quoted as he commented on how they played 'Black Night' at the gig that featured; "It's a bit fast. You see, on stage you tend to do things a bit faster than for a record, the occasion tends to excite you a little. This is the old arrangement, we don't do it anymore. This was probably recorded in Aachen last March or April at an open air concert. Actually, for a bootleg, it's not bad quality, there's reasonable balance."

H Bomb is an interesting example of what Deep Purple sounded like in the early days of MkII. In terms of the set list, there was certainly a hangover of songs from the MkI era, even when *In Rock* had been released. Ian Gillan stipulated; "With two new members to ease into the band, we rehearsed a lot. There was a need to balance early gigs with material written before my arrival, and new songs."

H Bomb features a long version of 'Wring That Neck' where a lot of solos and jams stretch it out but again, Deep Purple were exciting as a live band because audiences never knew what they were going to get. In this instance, there are some fascinating themes and variations on tunes such as 'In The Hall Of The Mountain King', 'Three Blind Mice' and 'Jingle Bells'. Well, as Jon Lord put it years later when addressing the fact that *Fireball* diverts from the musical focus set out with *In Rock*, "why not?".

Ritchie Blackmore was quoted in *The LA Times* in June 1974; "I have to be turned on by the audience. I like to show off. Whenever I get out on stage, I know I'm a great guitarist. I know I can blow any other guitarist off any stage. It all comes out. When I go in the studio, I think I'm playing to the engineer and a few other people. It doesn't do anything for me. It usually ends up okay, that's good enough. I know it won't get any better."

Jon Lord told *Record Mirror* in October 1970; "Live appearances are enormously important to bands today because audiences are far more discriminating and they are no longer satisfied with just recorded sounds. They seem to accept the fact that there can be two different experiences — inside and out of the recording studio."

Ritchie Blackmore said in *Disc & Music Echo* in October 1970; "You can sum up the whole audience reaction thing today by saying that excitement does not come from pretty faces any more, it comes from the music from your instruments. The problem with the Stones now is that they don't generate excitement from their instruments. Mick Taylor is a good guitarist but Mick Jagger is their only showman — and really the Stones haven't a good musical thing going. Audiences now are much more aware of the music — and maybe that's why groups like the Hollies have gone on. The musical excitement started with the Cream and Jimi Hendrix, and, to a lesser extent, the Who, who are not brilliant musicians but do give excitement. I like to think Deep Purple are an exciting band musically, but what gets the audience reaction is the showmanship that goes with it. There are hundreds of good guitarists in Britain but most of them are so boring to watch! I'm an introvert off stage so

Bootlegging

I love to jump about on stage. I suppose it's fifty per cent enjoying leaping about myself, and fifty per cent watching the audience leaping about! I'd far rather get the reaction, 'what a great show' than play musically for the heads. I've been through all that five years ago. But there are strange anomalies. Some nights I come off stage having played really well and there's been little reaction from the audience — and at other times I've played really badly and the reaction's been great. And I don't really know which is better. People will shout at me and say 'it's the music that counts, man' but if you ask me what was the best date I've played recently I'd say the Aachen Festival in Germany, when my amplifier caught fire and the whole stage went up in smoke. But maybe if you ask me that question again in five years time I'll pick out a date that was really good musically. So I suppose you'll have to say that Deep Purple do encourage active audience reaction — but we try not to let the music suffer as a result."

I have referred to the *H Bomb* bootleg because it is probably the most well-known one due to how widely it was distributed at the time. To put it in context on the MkII timeline, the date of the Aachen concert was during the same month that *In Rock* had been released. The content on *H Bomb* is basically reflective of the days when Deep Purple were still using MkI material during the live shows. It was quite a bit later down the line that *Fireball* material would feature in the live shows. All the same, it is very much worth listening to whatever bootlegs you can get hold of that document what Deep Purple sounded like live whilst they were riding high on the success of *In Rock* and working on *Fireball* in the background.

I advocate that it offers a tremendous amount of context in terms of the enthusiasm and power in all of the band's playing at the time. There is often a popular narrative, I find, among people who don't like *Fireball* (both fans and in particular, Ritchie Blackmore) that goes something like; "*Fireball* isn't very good because we were working too hard with the touring." For all the factors that may have been going against making the *Fireball* album though, when listening to the bootlegs that were made around that time, the content is certainly not reflective of a band who are on their last legs and playing terribly as a result, very much the opposite in fact!

Maybe it was down to the professionalism of the band and their

Deep Purple - Fireball: In-depth

ability and determination to put on a good performance regardless of how tired they were from the intensity of touring. Maybe it came down to the fact that Deep Purple sound considerably different live than in the studio (and have a pretty much shared philosophy that playing live often felt more innovative and exciting for them and indeed the audience). We will never truly know I suppose but my point is this; no matter what any member of Deep Purple or their fanbase might feel about *Fireball*, you'd be hard pushed to find fault with the quality and excitement in their live performances at that time (of course, ignoring the poor sound quality on some elements of some bootlegs because that's bootlegging for you. For instance, on the *H Bomb* bootleg, Ian Gillan's microphone was certainly giving him some trouble but take that out of the equation and his vocals in and of themselves are brilliant — strong, melodic and with feeling).

In December 1971, it was reported in *Sounds*; "Deep Purple, about to start recording a new album, are alarmed at the prospect that a bootleg album containing material intended for the album may be on the verge of release. The band's lead guitarist, Ritchie Blackmore, told *Sounds* that they had been informed of the existence of a completed bootleg containing at least two numbers intended for the next album. The band has played several new numbers at gigs and Blackmore thought that they may have been taped at one of these. 'We always keep a sharp lookout for tape recorders but we haven't seen any,' added Blackmore. Deep Purple's recording company, EMI, said on Monday that there was as yet no concrete proof that such a bootleg album did exist. 'If and when it does appear, action will be taken,' said a spokesman."

Of course, whilst bootlegging might not have been appreciated at the time, in the long run, it is probably the general opinion that most fans are very appreciative of the fact that it happened; bootlegging has resulted in wider illustration of what Deep Purple sounded like live at various points in their career and in terms of the *Fireball* studio album, bootlegs containing content from that era add so much context and understanding as to how and what Deep Purple were playing live around that time.

In July 2011 Roger Glover was quoted in *Goldmine*; "I could never understand our success; I could never understand why so many people bought our records, because they were so full of flaws! And then I started listening to bootlegs and to what we really were, and I came to reassess the whole thing. Listening to bootlegs from the early 1970s, I realised what a dangerous band we were, and how exciting it was not to know what was going to happen next. We walked a very thin line between chaos and order, and that was the magic, that was why people bought our records. I came from a pop band (Episode Six), and when you're a pop band, you learn the song, and you play it the same way every night. And now, there's this band veering off, and suddenly the solo's in E when it should be ... 'hey, what's happening here?' — that's the magic."

Bootlegs seem to fill some historic gaps that weren't covered by officially recorded material at the time. Perhaps the next best thing is concert reviews. Deep Purple's show at The Roundhouse in London that took place on 30th April was reviewed in *New Musical Express* in May 1971; "This could easily be a review consisting entirely of superlatives, but it wouldn't be so easy to understand unless you were actually at the Roundhouse on Friday night. Let it rest at this — Deep Purple left absolutely no doubt in my mind that they are just about the most exciting professional rock (and that includes rock and roll) group in the world. Playing to a packed house, Purple opened with 'Speed King', a very violent number which had lead guitarist Ritchie Blackmore spinning round and vocalist Ian Gillan assaulting the mic stand. It was an amazing opening number; the sheer force of the music was practically breathtaking — Ian Paice driving it all along with beautiful rock drumming. 'Strange Kind Of Woman' was a much longer version than the single and had Ritchie demonstrating his technique. During this number Ian sings the notes that Ritchie plays at one stage, it's an example of perfect co-ordination and voice control. Ian went off stage as usual during the excellent 'Child In Time' and Jon, little Ian, Roger and Ritchie fell into a perfectly matched free-for-all, Ritchie leaning against his amps with a roadie holding them up, Roger, in hat and clogs, belting away, Jon underlying everything that was going on by playing excellent organ and excellent electric piano and little Ian contributing so much. Jon's sense of humour came through when he launched into Bach's *Toccata And Fugue*, switched to 'Gurney Slade' and then began 'Mandrake

Root' which Ritchie particularly wanted to include. The fans were ecstatically pleased with the concert and they showed it. Purple were brought back for an encore which turned out to be 'Black Night' with a false introduction. Ian Gillan's rock and roll upbringing became obvious when, after insistent applause, Purple performed 'Lucille'. He is a master exciter and the showmanship that had been obvious all evening became even more apparent. In the dressing room after the show, all five members of the group were completely flaked out — they had given the audience something to remember."

Of course, there is the *Scandinavian Nights* album; that documents Deep Purple's pre *Fireball* live set, but it wasn't made available as an official recording until 1988 and thus, at the time, it was only really *H Bomb* that was available as a reference to what Deep Purple sounded like live at the time that *Fireball* was released. The content on *Scandinavian Nights* was recorded in the Stockholm Konserthuset on 12th November 1970. The recording was originally made by Swedish National Radio for a radio show called *Tonkraft*. It is a good example of the early MkII set list comprising of songs from *In Rock* and long instrumentals from earlier albums. As with *H Bomb*, 'Mandrake Root' and 'Wring that Neck' account for the majority of the material in the set list. It wasn't until the *Fireball* tour that Deep Purple began to add more original material.

Certainly, in favour of *Fireball*, it saw additions to the MkII live set list that would go on to become iconic. *Made In Japan* springs to mind here. Roger Glover was quoted in *New Musical Express* in October 1972; "We recorded every show in Japan for an album to be released over there but now we're thinking of putting it out in Britain too. There are so many bootlegs of us going around. If we put out our own live set, it should kill their market. Ours would be a double album and we'd like to bring it out at just over the normal price of a single album."

Roger Glover was quoted in the same interview as he explained the way in which he hoped that *Made In Japan* would discourage bootleggers; "Being bootlegged can really be a drag. All groups have good and bad nights and if they catch you on a bad gig then the record can really turn people off. They hear it and think 'Christ, Deep Purple aren't much good' I've found this myself. I heard a Led Zeppelin

Bootlegging

bootleg and they sounded terrible, it's just not fair on the bands, it's a rotten business. It happened in Germany a lot, a couple of years ago. You'd see the millions of mics on little stands, sticking up from the audience. Our roadies went out and grabbed all the tapes they could and got into a few fights but there's really very little you can do about it. We had a court case against Virgin Records, which we won. That stopped them selling our bootlegs, but it's a drag. The live album from Japan could kill the market, that would be a great thing. Another reason for wanting to put it out is that the stage act we've been using on the British tour will be dropped next year. The next one will be based around the new album, although of course there will be some old songs because people always want to hear them."

Bearing in mind that *Made In Japan* was the first official release of what Deep Purple MkII sounded like in the context of a live gig, ironically, that probably adds historic value to the content on the bootlegs that were recorded prior to that and feature the live sets as they were at the time.

It was considered by some that when *Fireball* was Deep Purple's most recent album, there was more to be said for the live shows they were doing at the time than the album itself. As was written in a review of their performance at Felt Forum in New York in *Cashbox* in November 1971; "It takes time, and there's no other way to look at it. 'Hush'. Even that took time. It's a system, like any other system — and you either become part of it or it destroys you. Entirely. There's only one way to win — and that is to endure. To watch those around you being destroyed and to be inspired by their destruction. Deep Purple was inspired. They are six albums old (three of them on the now defunct Tetragrammaton label and three with Warner Bros.), and are still learning. There's strength in numbers, and to be strong, they have learned to stay together. They are five. But on stage, they act and perform as a single, tightly knit unit whose years of rehearsals and disappointments have finally paid off. They are professional. Deep Purple can do it all — from hard rock to classical music, and they do it exceptionally well. There is no front man who immediately steals the attention of the audience, but rather five individuals who share in the glory. Ian Gillan, who gained international recognition via his incredible performance as Christ, is

Deep Purple - Fireball: In-depth

by far the best vocalist to have emerged in the music industry. Period. For strange as it may seem, Ian Gillan can sing, really sing. Ritchie Blackmore, guitarist, spins like a top in flight while attacking his guitar much in the same manner as Hendrix. For the most part, he's a tasty guitarist whose speed is used advantageously. Ian Paice and Roger Glover comprise the Deep Purple rhythm section and create a fine driving background for Jon Lord's organ work. Deep Purple has changed over the many years. They moved from the commercial AM audiences into the Royal Philharmonic where they were lost for a time but recovered only to find themselves immersed in the hard rock sound. Their Philharmonic album, probably the best they've ever done, was totally overlooked both by the listening audiences and by critics — but still Deep Purple endured. With the release of *Fireball* (a cheap duplicate of their earlier *Deep Purple In Rock* album), Deep Purple had arrived — and were here to stay. They will in the next year, emerge as just another British supergroup, but their talents far surpass those of their predecessors."

It could be advocated that the reviewer was being pretty darn derogatory towards *Fireball* but the fact remains that it happened and was an opinion shared by many, including some members of Deep Purple.

Chapter Six
Babyface And Other Projects

Deep Purple's last UK tour date after the UK release of *Fireball* was in Southampton. Less than two weeks later in October 1971 in America, Ian Gillan was struck down with hepatitis. The rest of the tour was cancelled immediately and as a result, Deep Purple were pretty much dormant for a number of months. As journalist, Dick Meadows, reported in *Sounds* in December 1971; "Purple were set to go to North America this month until vocalist Ian Gillan was stricken with hepatitis. For a time he was very ill and the tour was postponed until January. Now Ian is recovering but is still weak. In the meantime the band has been taking things comparatively easily; the only time they get to rest is when one of their number is ill. Otherwise they work themselves to a standstill."

With time to look into other ideas and options, Blackmore booked studio time back at De Lane Lea. Ian Paice came with him to what came to be known as the Babyface sessions. Blackmore had apparently taken note of Phil Lynott's talents when he had seen him play at a gig during the summer. At the time, Thin Lizzy were yet to become a high-profile band. The Babyface sessions actually took place prior to Thin Lizzy having their first hit single, 'Whiskey In The Jar'. However, Thin Lizzy were certainly well respected among other musicians; they had done two albums already that had received critical acclaim.

Thin Lizzy's manager, Chris O'Donnell was very displeased about the whole Babyface thing. Understandable really as in, Lynott would go on to be an asset to Thin Lizzy and O'Donnell obviously wanted him there. Ritchie Blackmore recalled the session in *The Guardian* in April 2015; "I wanted to leave with Ian (Paice) at the time because we'd both had enough. I am a very sensitive kind of

Deep Purple - Fireball: In-depth

person, believe it or not. I was working too hard and couldn't take the strain... Ian and I were gonna form another band with Phil Lynott from Thin Lizzy, actually. It was like Hendrix number two. He looked like Hendrix, sounded like Hendrix."

Dick Meadows reported in *Sounds* in December 1971; During their enforced lay-off, organist Jon Lord has been working with Tony Ashton, bassist Roger Glover has been doing some producing, and Ritchie and "Little" Ian Paice, the drummer, have been playing with a third guy — who Ritchie won't identify — as a rock trio. They have put down some songs and one will be released as a single in the new year under a name that gives no clue to its Deep Purple heritage."

It's funny really, on the one hand there seems to be this narrative of "give the band a break from all that touring and the pressure to release a new album each year" and yet, when Deep Purple had to have a break due to Ian Gillan having hepatitis, none of the other members seemed to want to take advantage of the opportunity to have a rest. Maybe it was a case of them wanting to keep other doors open at the time or perhaps it was the obvious action that any career musician would take. Still though, it is fascinating to think that as much as everyone in Deep Purple may have felt very overworked at the time of *Fireball* being made, there was very little done by anyone to take some time out, except when it was forced on them by their own illness from overdoing it. Ironic in its way really.

Genuinely though, the fact that each band member was keen to embrace other projects whilst Deep Purple was on a brief break due to Gillan's hepatitis is easily suggestive of how everyone concerned was keen to keep their options open as in, at the time, the future of Deep Purple perhaps didn't look as secure as it ultimately came to be (it's 2021 and they're still going with Roger Glover, Ian Gillan, Ian Paice and then Don Airey on keyboards and Steve Morse on guitar).

In the same *Sounds* feature, Dick Meadows seemed to hint at a lack of stability within Deep Purple; "The inevitable fragmentation during Gillan's illness perhaps provides a clue to the future. Individual members of the band are inclined towards virtuosity on stage — Blackmore admits he is an egotist when playing — and they are eager to solo and take their fair share of acclaim. Whether they can continue to get sufficient personal satisfaction is doubtful, although obviously they're not anxious to destroy the huge success story that has taken a long while to write. Nevertheless there have been musical clashes within the band in the past. Lord, for instance, is keen on merging rock with classics. Blackmore wants to remain more exclusively in rock."

The possibility of Babyface releasing a single remained in sight even after *Machine Head* had been released. It was reported in *Melody Maker* in May 1972; "Ritchie is taking his time over his solo project which may reach fruition by Christmas. Already he has written material which is not for Purple, and made tapes with Ian Paice at the drums and a bassist/vocalist from another group who wishes to remain nameless."

Of course, it is now known that this was the Babyface project. It's understandable that Phil Lynott wasn't named at the time though — it was probably too messy to do considering how it could have compromised his chances with Thin Lizzy, particularly seeing as at the time, the band were on the brink of making it really big.

As Blackmore continued in the same interview; "It's coming on very slowly, but I want to be sure about it. It's a sort of rock/blues band, very different from Purple. I would like to make a single with them because that's the quickest way to get things going, but they wouldn't play our kind of stuff on the radio. We have got a couple of tracks down and I am pretty pleased with them. I want to do something where it is all my own fault if it goes wrong, or my own fault if it turns out good. After Christmas it may be the turning point for Purple. We are having a good time but it's got to end sometime. Jon is doing his own things and Roger is into production. I just think there is room for more excitement in today's music and I want to do something about it. I think I can do something more exciting than Deep Purple. Although we are all good musicians in Purple, we are limited to certain things. It's hard to write hard riffs all the time. I don't think we can get much bigger than we are at the moment and it's a nice position to be in. But it can't last for ever."

Blackmore was quoted in March 1972 in *Disc & Music Echo*; "I want to get on with my band — we all want to get on with our other interests — and I have to envisage an end to Deep Purple to stay sane. But we'll keep together for a bit yet because we're earning good money and we might as well clean up — I think we deserve it. I starved for six years, and the band has built itself a good reputation over the years."

Roger Glover said in the Drew Thompson produced 2014 documentary, *Deep Purple: Made In Japan*; "Although we were wildly successful with *Deep Purple In Rock* and *Fireball*, we actually hadn't made much money because we were paying back the management for having funded the band for so many years. So despite all that success, we needed to make some money.".

The Babyface recordings never saw the light of day. Perhaps they were too primitive. Maybe there was some kind of pact to keep them a secret for whatever reason. Oh well, had Babyface taken off, Ritchie Blackmore's career could have gone in a very different direction (no Rainbow?!), as could Deep Purple's have done. For all fans who like all of Deep Purple's post *Fireball* albums, maybe it's just as well. Ian Paice was quoted in *Classic Rock* in May 2018; "Deep Purple constructed music in a very specific way. Limiting isn't the word, but it was a little more arranged. Ritchie and I thought it would be fun to have the freedom of a three-piece band, where basically everything was up for grabs musically — you could change every song every night, which we couldn't really do in Purple. We'd see Phil Lynott with Thin Lizzy at the Speakeasy club in London really early on in their career, and we thought, 'Wow, what a fantastic voice' but we didn't actually pay a lot of attention to his bass playing, because he was such a great vocalist. So we thought we'd try something out — me, Ritchie and him. We got a day together in a studio in Holland Park in West London, and we just started to mess around to see what happened. We started jamming some new stuff and seeing what happened, which is what we do with Purple anyway, though obviously the Purple set-up was very different. The stuff we were jamming was bluesier (sic), more in a Cream or Free vein, that kind of idea. Well, Phil's voice was staggering, wonderful. But he couldn't play, at least not to the standard that we needed if it was just Ritchie, myself and a bass. When there's only three of you, everybody's got to be really good on everything they do. Really, the bass playing had to be on a par with someone like Jack Bruce. And, God bless him, Phil wasn't there yet. He was pretty simple, and quite often out of tune and out of time. And although he became really, really good at everything he did, at that point he wasn't. Ritchie and I looked at each other and went 'It's not working. It's a nice attempt to try and do this three-piece thing, but let's go and rethink it' but we never did rethink it. We got back on the road with Purple and it just sort of disappeared into the mist. I saw Phil a couple of times after that, but it was always really in passing ('Hey, how you doing? Gotta go. Bye bye.') but the ship had sailed by that time. We actually recorded the session. The tapes got lost somewhere along the line, but really there was nothing to it. We didn't even bother mixing it. It just wasn't happening."

Ritchie Blackmore told *Sounds* in February 1974; "I wanted to get my own band together, with Phil Lynott and Ian Paice because we've always stuck together. We thought we'll get this together and start again more or less. I asked Jon what he was doing. He was going to go with Tony Ashton and I said I'm of to make a rock band like Deep Purple and Paice is coming with me. Ian (Paice) said it would be silly to abandon our years' efforts. I thought it would be an adventure, but finally agreed that it would be silly starting from scratch."

It wasn't just Blackmore who was doing other things during Deep Purple's enforced hiatus in 1971 though. Other projects were a commonality with all members of the band and when Blackmore came down with hepatitis in 1972, touring got delayed once again which inevitably, freed up time for the rest of Deep Purple to pursue other things.

In *Beat Instrumental* in June 1972, Roger Glover contributed as a guest writer; "It seems that every article written about Deep Purple these days is a hard luck story. The unfortunate thing is that it's true. We do seem to have had an incredible amount of bad luck in the past six months. The frustrating thing is that there is absolutely nothing we can do about it except have all our shots before every tour and then hope we make it. For anyone who doesn't know, Ritchie caught hepatitis and yellow jaundice in America (as did Ian Gillan last year), and so we had to cancel what appeared to be our best tour to date (same as last year). However, bad luck is not all there is to think about. On the record side of our career, things seem to be going

Deep Purple - Fireball: In-depth

very well. I hope I haven't spoken too soon, but *Machine Head* is already the most successful album we've had in the States, and is fast catching up with *Deep Purple In Rock* here (UK) and in Europe. In the meantime, we've been doing a bit of work and a bit of relaxing. Apart from going over to Dublin with Jon to collect an award for being the top progressive group of 1971, in a poll, I've been messing around in studios. Rupert Hine, whose album I produced last year for Purple Records, has written, with his lyricist David McIver, a song called 'Hamburgers' which, it is hoped, will be a single very shortly. We did it at Air Studios with John Punter, and I'm really happy with the way it's turned out. I just hope *Radio One* likes it half as much. A few days ago, Dave Cousins of The Strawbs phoned me up and said he was wondering whether I'd be interested in some session work. Of course I said yes, especially as Deep Purple weren't working at the time. He came round the house and talked about the music over a few pints. It seems that he is making a solo album and wanted a different set of musicians to those he is used to working with. And so I find myself at The Manor (a big old manor house in Oxfordshire, with a sixteen track studio built in) with Millar Anderson on guitar, me on bass, Jon Hiseman on drums and of course, Dave on acoustic guitar. Rick Wakeman is rumoured to be arriving soon. It's quite refreshing to be playing bass in such an obviously different style of music to Deep Purple and Dave has written some really fine songs. Anyway, we'll be back on the road as soon as Ritchie is fit."

The success of *Concerto For Group And Orchestra* was such that Jon Lord was commissioned to write a follow up; *Gemini Suite* consisted of five movements that were inspired by each member of Deep Purple. The suite was performed live in September 1970 by The Light Music Society Orchestra at the Royal Festival Hall and it was then recorded as a studio project in 1971 by the London Symphony Orchestra conducted by Malcolm Arnold. *Gemini Suite* was an important step for Jon Lord because it functioned as a continuation of his musical aspirations outside of Deep Purple.

Gemini Suite paved the way for his later projects, *Windows* in 1974, *Sarabande* in 1975 and *Before I Forget* in 1982. As was reported in *Record Mirror* in October 1970; "Jon Lord is collaborating with Tony Ashton on the score for the movie, *The Last Rebel*."

Babyface And Other Projects

Although Deep Purple as a unit had established that after *Concerto For Group And Orchestra*, the desired direction for the band was in rock (it is rumoured that this is how the first MkII studio album got its name), as an individual, Jon Lord's interest in working with orchestras and taking his creativity in a more classically inspired direction is something that always remained.

He was quoted in *The Guardian* in June 1971; "I've been incredibly lucky but sometimes it's awfully difficult when people say, 'what do you want to be?' I tell them I want to be a composer... The reaction from the rock world has been pretty generous. After the concerto people got quite excited. It was the first thing that had worked in terms of audience. I sometimes feel this guarded response — 'here's a rock musician who wants to be a composer' — you get it from something like the London Symphony Orchestra, but then you talk to them and they find out you're not a dummy."

In the same interview, when asked to define what success meant to him, Lord said; "For me it's freedom, to take my time and to end up doing what I want to do." Jon Lord's passion for orchestral music really came across in his interview with *The Guardian*; "As a writer of orchestral music — which I'm not yet, but which I want to be — I'm much more pleased with the new piece. *The Concerto For Group And Orchestra* had one foot in the nineteenth century, half accidentally and half deliberately and *Gemini* struggles a bit harder into the twentieth century. It was such a thing to work with the London Symphony Orchestra. It sounds silly to say it but, you know, they're such a great orchestra. To have them playing something of mine was an incredible experience, I just wish it could happen every week... I'm always trying to prevent myself falling into the romanticism trap, but the night my daughter Sara was born, I wrote the violin theme of the slow movement of the *Gemini Suite*. My wife Judith insisted that I should be present, and afterwards I went home all teary-eyed and wrote it."

The orchestra stuff was definitely a Jon Lord thing. That's not surprising really considering that he was a classically trained pianist who had completed his musical training and the related examinations. In *Melody Maker* in March 1971 he said; "I still think the fusion of a group and orchestra has validity, if only for entertainment. And

Deep Purple - Fireball: In-depth

in fact I am working on a solo project this week with the London Symphony Orchestra. We are recording my *Gemini Suite* at the EMI Studios in London."

In June 1974, Blackmore was quoted in *The LA Times*; "I love classical music, I don't like rock musicians playing with classical orchestras. I thought it was stupid when we were doing it. I still think it's stupid. The two styles are never integrated." And in *Guitar International* in 1975 he commented; "I didn't like that (*Concerto For Group And Orchestra*). I didn't like the way it was written. It was like rock band meets orchestra and it was more of a battle instead of being integrated. It wasn't integrated one bit as far as I was concerned. The orchestra played badly, too. They didn't particularly excel themselves. And, I like an orchestra playing orchestral works, not playing rock 'n' roll."

Of course, evidently, Blackmore embraced the opportunity to play with orchestras later on in his career, as is the case on the *Rainbow Rising* album (1976) and live performances of 'Difficult To Cure' during the early eighties. At the time of *Fireball* and indeed his interviews in 1974 and 1975 though, not wanting to play with orchestras anymore was Blackmore's stance on the matter at the time.

Something that I find really fascinating is that with regards to *Fireball* there seems to be two very conflicting narratives present. On the one hand, there's this whole thing surrounding the album where it is complained that an extensive and intense touring schedule was to blame for *Fireball* not being everything that it could have been and yet, here we have a group of five individuals who, illness accounted for, were all active in embracing projects outside of Deep Purple during periods that the band was forced to take a break due to said illness. So I'm looking at all the resources here and I'm thinking, "well, did they want some time off or didn't they?".

Besides, a hectic schedule was not exclusive to just *Fireball* as in, *In Rock* was subject to some of the same so-called pitfalls. Both albums were recorded alongside touring schedules and therefore in different studios. Band members were committed to other projects during the making of both albums (Ian Gillan recorded his vocal part for *Jesus Christ Superstar* not long after he had joined Deep Purple; The album was recorded from October 1969 to April 1970. It went to number one in the US on 20th February 1971. It had been climbing the *Billboard* albums chart since December 1970 and it spent over a year in it in total).

Also, this is a very subjective thing and there will never be a way of truly knowing the answers (I suspect even Deep Purple themselves would probably struggle to answer this one), but I wonder if it is possible that although with hindsight, Deep Purple and indeed their fans consider that the turbulence during the making of *Fireball* compromised the album and yet, whilst it was being made, there did seem to be a sense of optimism.

Not long before *Fireball* was due for release in the States, Blackmore was quoted in *Record Mirror* in May 1971; "We've already thrown out five songs on this album and it has cost at least £6,000 so far, but we are not going to start compromising the standards we have set with *In Rock* and if the result is another album with the longevity of that, which it will be, who is going to complain? The ideal way might be to rehearse or work the material out beforehand for most groups, but it just doesn't happen for us like that. Quite often we might arrive at the studios with no idea what we are going to do — at present there is no time to prepare anything anyway, but the fact is that it is the spontaneity of our music which lends it vitality and excitement."

Roger Glover seemed to express a similar optimism a month prior to *Fireball*'s US release when he told *New Musical Express* in June 1971; "Our present average is one album and two singles a year, it could be two albums and three singles a year. I think we should record more. One big criticism I've got of the group is that we should put more product, more good product, on the market."

Glover continued; "Producing is something I've wanted to do for a long time. Producing is the next thing to being a musician for me. I've been pretty ill and I can't see me lasting on the road for, at a conservative estimate, more than another three years, so obviously I must look to the future. It's such a difference to being a producer to being a musician. When you get people you know and respect coming up to you for advice it's quite a mind-blower. I shan't be a producer from now on though, it's just a one-off thing. But it stands you in good stead for the future."

Deep Purple - Fireball: In-depth

Of course, it emerged that producing wasn't a one-time thing for Glover and rightly so — because he has producing credits on Nazareth, Rory Gallagher and Rainbow albums where he has done a fantastic job of it. During some time off from Deep Purple, Roger Glover and Ian Paice went to Atlanta, Georgia to produce the debut album for the band, Elf. If it wasn't for this occurrence, it is possible that vocalist, Ronnie James Dio, may not have been introduced to Deep Purple and ultimately Ritchie Blackmore when Elf ended up supporting Deep Purple on future tours. Subtly, it's strange to think that were it not for the haphazard days of a cancelled tour after *Fireball*'s UK release, the music history concerning all members of Deep Purple could have gone on to look very different indeed.

Really, in many ways, it's phenomenal that (line-up changes accounted for) Deep Purple managed to stay together at all. The instances in which band members were thinking of a career outside of the group continued long after the tumultuous days of *Fireball*. Jon Lord was quoted in an interview with *Sounds* in February 1973; "Ritchie and I are poles apart, in what we want to end up producing and what we want an end product to be. Deep Purple is that conflict. Like, Ritchie will come up with a really raunchy hard riff and a way of playing a number and then we find that when we've got to rehearse, there is no room for the organ. It is just pure heavy metal guitar so we have to mould it to fit the other people in the band. I'm pretty certain that Ritchie wants to make a solo album with just guitar, drums and bass because he feels that it is a side of him that will be presented far better that way. I want to make an album because I believe in some of the songs I write. It's not necessarily going to produce a band, it's going to produce an album and then we'll see what happens... I also want to play a lot more piano because I was originally a pianist and I do still love playing it."

Seemingly though, there was perhaps just something about being in Deep Purple that was difficult to walk away from. In the same interview, Lord was quoted; "I've got very vague ideas about what I want to do when Deep Purple has finished, but when you're in something like Deep Purple, you see it as very difficult to stop it because you find you are contracted for years. I mean, I write a lot of songs which we don't use in the band because they are not Deep

Babyface And Other Projects

Purple. A band is a band and it has an established identity and it can't change that identity overnight. I mean, you wouldn't expect Humble Pie to suddenly do 'My Way' or Deep Purple to do a song on the album that I've just recorded with Tony Ashton."

Ian Gillan recalled; "Recovery from (hepatitis) gave me the chance to look at life and try to find some kind of focus and sense of perspective and, as did the rest of the guys, I went into solo projects, including the producing of an album for a band called Jerusalem and the development of a children's musical called *Cherkazoo*. We were still in Deep Purple, with a major programme ahead, but the cracks were there, both with management and each other."

Cherkazoo was eventually released as an album in 1992. It featured eight tracks from a children's story that Gillan wrote songs around circa 1972. The second part of the album consists of songs that were most likely recorded sometime around 1974, not long after Gillan's departure from Deep Purple. A cover of Elvis Presley's 'Trying To Get You' is included. The line-ups for both sessions on the *Cherkazoo* album have never been confirmed. According to the album's liner notes, it is possible that Roger Glover played bass. I think this is plausible based on how Glover spoke of a project that he was working on with Gillan.

Roger Glover said in *New Musical Express* in October 1972; "When we were in Episode Six we wrote a pile of songs together. Ian (Gillan) took the best of them and has wound them into an idea for a film. We've been putting down some of the songs to see what they sound like and so that we can play them to producers. It's gonna be quite a big thing. At the moment they're just demos to give people an idea of what we have in mind. Ian has a definite idea but we don't want to discuss it yet — someone might pinch it. It could turn out well, but really it's just a little thing we're working at on the side. We're messing around in a way, but I'm knocked out with it. I think it's really good."

Luckily, Gillan's recovery, despite him ignoring doctor's orders to rest for longer, resulted in Deep Purple being able to regroup and then go on to make their next album, *Machine Head*.

Deep Purple - Fireball: In-depth

Chapter Seven
Machine Head Saves The Day?

Ritchie Blackmore was quoted in *New Musical Express* in September 1971; "I think we're gonna get through as much work as possible, though personally I think it's a bit too much. The main thing is getting the next album done, living in little huts in the Swiss mountains. I'm hoping the next one will be a little better."

Bearing in mind that this interview took place the same month that *Fireball* was released in the UK, it appears that Blackmore was certain in his disappointment with *Fireball* even before there had really been enough time to see what the UK reviews made of it. Journalist, Julie Webb, reported in *New Musical Express* in February 1972; "After a bad patch towards the end of '71 — when lead singer Ian Gillan was ordered to rest, and the band had to cancel an American tour — Deep Purple are back again. They've completed a short tour and almost ready is their next album, *Machine Head*, expected to release in March."

Ritchie Blackmore recalled to *Sounds* in February 1974; "I had hepatitis, Ian had hepatitis and it gave us time to think about songs, and we all got together in the writing and *Machine Head* was a step up." Roger Glover was quoted in *New Musical Express* in June 1971; "We just don't mean that much in America, that's why we've got to go over there."

Okay, so picture the scene as it may have looked at the time. The first three Deep Purple albums with the first line-up of the band had been a bit hit and miss internationally, overall. *In Rock* came along with the second line-up of Deep Purple and had the fantastically exciting impact of a heavy metal wrecking ball and then, oh, er... *Fireball*. Imagine what could have happened if it wasn't for *Machine Head* coming after *Fireball*. If we're to take the generally held opinion

Deep Purple - Fireball: In-depth

(rightly or wrongly) that *In Rock* was a bigger deal than *Fireball*, at least commercially, if it wasn't for *Machine Head* being generally considered the turning point for much improvement then well, who knows! I personally suspect that had *Machine Head* underwhelmed Deep Purple and their listeners overall in the same way that *Fireball* had, it is plausible that the motive to make another album might have been significantly diminished (actually, come to think of it, *Who Do We Think We Are* was generally not well regarded by Deep Purple or their fans but there are many sources suggestive of the fact that such problem was down to personnel difficulties at the time rather than any particular lack of belief in Deep Purple, both from the band's founding members and the fans).

Fireball seemed to have quite the effect on morale for Ritchie Blackmore. As he was quoted in March 1972 in *Disc & Music Echo*; "Four months ago I'd have said that the band was past its best work, now I know that it isn't. When Ian was sick we had about two months to write and it shows on this latest album. But I personally don't think I've given the people, or myself, anything which I feel very proud of. It's very weird, you get this frustrated feeling, you know what you want to do but you don't know how to put it across — that's why I formed my three-piece band on the side. There's five people in Deep Purple and you can never do the music you want to do one hundred per cent, so it's compromise all the way down the line. It has to be with five virtuosos in the band, I don't think there's one of us who could say 'that's *my* music' — most of the stuff is written by Roger and myself with the words and melody done by Ian. I personally would like an outlet and to hear a record done exactly like I imagine it played in the first place. It gets distorted from my original version in the studio."

In some ways, it comes across that Ritchie Blackmore has been prone to worrying about getting things right throughout his career. We'll never know, that's his business but certainly, on the month that *Machine Head* was released, he was quoted in an interview with *Disc & Music Echo* in March 1972 that was suggestive of the fact that he was keen for things to go well; "I worry too much really, I get a lot of tellings off from the management. If you're an emotional type of person like I am, you just get upset about any little thing — the lights

Machine Head Saves The Day

aren't right, the stage isn't right. So I have to make sure I get there early to see if the hall's all right. And I can't play unless I've walked round the hall first. I go out front while the first group is playing and look at the audience, and I weigh up the amount of echo because you can't do fast runs if there's too much. Then I'll go back into the dressing room and say, 'there's not a musical lot out there tonight' or 'they're quiet, they want music.' I have to do all this because if there's the smallest thing wrong it changes my whole way of thinking and it's nagging at me so I can't concentrate on the music... They (an audience in Denmark) were screaming and jumping up on stage, whereas in Germany in the north it was entirely the opposite, and in England it's about a happy medium. Germany is disappointing for us at the moment. For the last year and a half we've been number one, we've sold more records there than the Beatles. When we play in the south it goes a bomb, in the north they just sit there. I think they expect us to fly on stage or something. The terrible thing is, that I think they think we're very arrogant. Last time, I went to shake a girl's hand across the barriers at the front to show we were a bit human, and she just shrank away — I felt terribly embarrassed... I don't get stage fright much now, only if I know there's close relatives in the audience. Usually you can treat the people as a mass, but if you know your brother or your mother or your wife is there then it makes you frightened. It's written into our contract that there must be two bottles of whisky and twenty-eight bottles of coke in the dressing room for us. We have to have something before we go on stage. In our case we have to have something that lifts us up — we're fairly heavy drinkers."

I trust that many fans would have enjoyed it when Blackmore gigged in his home county. The *Weston Mercury & Somerset Herald* reviewed a show that took place on 14th March 1970 at Weston-super-Mare Winter Gardens Pavilion; "One of the country's leading groups of pop musicians, Deep Purple, are the stars of Saturday Scene at the Winter Gardens Pavilion this evening. When they last appeared here in October, they were acclaimed for their musical versatility and Weston pop fans can expect another polished performance from Deep Purple tomorrow."

As journalist, Dick Meadows, reported in *Sounds* in December

Deep Purple - Fireball: In-depth

1971; "The anatomy of a heavy rock band in today's pop society is a complex one. The sweat and toil reaps rewards in terms of enormous audience adulation and financial profit. But there is a difficult cross to bear at the same time and that is to be branded whipping boys in rock. Led Zeppelin and Ten Years After have become almost institutions whose stature has lifted them above the bitching. At the other end of the scale Sabbath and Uriah Heep are down there in the muck-raking mire nailed to this cross by critics. That the cross seems to be made of pound notes and fan hysteria obviously makes it more bearable. Just about balancing the see-saw of respect and smears is Deep Purple who have laboured for four years to achieve a mountain of success but still get slagged off rightly or wrongly for allegedly playing stereotype, formula rock."

This is what I mean when I say that in the days of *Fireball* being Deep Purple's most recent album, there was still this culture of them being the new boys. They were not big or successful enough to be secure in their careers (as a band or as individuals). There could easily have been a bit of a sword of Damocles thing going on in terms of how, they hadn't made it yet; they still had yet to secure their reputation in rock history. When making *Fireball*, the pressure would have been on not only due to the intensity of the touring and album release schedules at that time but also because they had yet to secure a reputation and thus career longevity as a band.

Ritchie Blackmore said in *Sounds* in December 1971; "We tend to consider what will please an audience. We think of that first and then what will please us perhaps second. So sometimes we get put down for playing fairly simple riffs. But you have got to consider the people you are playing for. That's what it is all about. King Crimson, for instance, turn out some very good stuff. I like things they do but what happens is that a lot of it goes over people's heads. Yes, we take criticism to heart but our attitude is not to talk about it too much. If we kept talking about what people were saying and what some reader from East Grinstead has written in a letter to a music paper then it would have a bad effect. We'd always be thinking, 'Are we doing the right thing?' It's funny really, some people have such closed minds about Purple and other groups as well. When you are coming up there is encouragement but the same people who have encouraged

Machine Head Saves The Day

you will then knock you down when you get some kind of success. Uriah Heep are having this happen to them, and they don't deserve all the criticism. You know, John Peel won't play us. He says we play formula rock and that's that. I don't know where that man is at any more. I did once but not now. Have you heard some of the people he is playing now? And people he has helped build up, he has turned his back on."

Yep, it seems to be pretty evident that not long after *Fireball*'s release, Deep Purple were still very much in the infancy of their success. They were still finding their feet in some ways and their relationship with the media and audiences alike seemed to be very touch and go. Sensibly, in the same interview Blackmore pragmatically advised; "Let people hear it and maybe like it, rather than pick up the record and say, 'Oh that's Deep Purple, don't like it and won't play it'."

As Dick Meadows considered in *Sounds* in December 1971 as he surmised Blackmore's opinion on Deep Purple's work up to that point; "The lead guitarist reckons *Deep Purple In Rock* is the finest thing they have done on record. It showed them going in one clear direction which they weren't before and that includes *Concerto For Group And Orchestra*. Which way they go now remains to be seen. It promises to be a significant fifth year for the band."

In *Sounds* in December 1971, Ritchie Blackmore was quoted as he expressed his disappointment with *Fireball*. It certainly seems that he was pinning his hopes on (the already titled at the time) *Machine Head* and that there was perhaps a feeling of make or break at the time; "This next album will show what Purple's future really is. I personally didn't like the last one, *Fireball*, too much, but this one I think will really get to the people. With *Fireball* we virtually made everything up in the studio, 'give us a riff' — that sort of thing. We were working so hard that we never had any time to sit back and think of new ideas for the album. There are only three tracks I think are good. 'No No No', 'Fools' and 'Fireball' itself."

It is important to remember though that *In Rock* and *Machine Head* were not (and possibly are not!) the holy grail of Deep Purple albums for every single member of the band. Generally, Ian Gillan has spoken more highly of *Fireball* in comparison to the other albums made during the first phase of the MkII line-up.

Gillan was quoted in *Sounds* in March 1976; "I decided I'd never come to the point where I would have to compromise my artistic feelings, it was getting to the point where Purple records were being churned out. We started off as progressive rock and there was no way we were a progressive rock band by *Who Do We Think We Are?*. I think it was laziness, fear. There was a difference in thought and attitude. There was a discrepancy in thought. I thought that *Fireball* was a great progression. After *Fireball* I felt we lapsed back into formulated music. *Machine Head* was like harking back to *In Rock*, everything was the same formula. It was a shame really because there was so much talent in that band. I left Purple because I was bored, I was bored with the same old thing. I found myself pacing the shows."

Still though, it seems that Gillan wasn't negating the extent to which *In Rock* was iconic. In the same interview, he was quoted; "I suppose out of all the Purple songs, if somebody was to pick out a song which was my particular thing in Purple then I suppose they'd pick out 'Child In Time', 'cause I suppose it was more me than anything else I did with Purple."

Equally, not long after *Machine Head* had been released, Jon Lord seemed to be keen to explore new musical territory rather than relying on the same tried and tested approach for the next album. He was quoted in April 1972 in *Sounds*; "To me, *Machine Head* (the new album) is the apex of what we started to do with *Deep Purple In Rock*, and I don't really think we should carry on along quite the same line. I think we should try and go round a few corners with the next one. Some people say about the group, probably with some justification, that we don't seem to have progressed very far since *Deep Purple In Rock*, though certainly inwardly each musician has progressed enormously — the writing talents have improved, our way of working together has improved, and we've got a much better working relationship between ourselves and with an audience. But where some of that justification lies is in the fact that we haven't really deviated from the very set line, and I think it's time we started to shoot for the stars a little bit more."

Lord was quoted in the same feature as he rationalised about how stepping outside the obvious confines of typical rock was something that he was keen to explore; "My feeling has always been that with our tempos — the speeds we use and the kind of rhythms we choose for our numbers, could be a little more inventive. I think we've sometimes underestimated the ability of our audience — the people that like us — to accept something a little bit more. Just because people like quote unquote, Hard Rock, it doesn't mean it has to be in 4/4 or a shuffle. The talents of the band are equal to far more than we're doing, while not putting down what we've done on the last three albums, and we've learnt a lot in that time. But I think we could now extend our boundaries a little bit. That doesn't mean that we should do something in 5/4 just for the sake of doing it in 5/4, but we shouldn't throw out the possibility of using different times and styles, bent to our own style."

Lord told *Sounds* in April 1972; "The trouble is that when you've got five people in a band you're going to get five different ideas of what's going to be good for the band's career. But for instance I'd think it would be excellent for our career to show a reasonably significant movement in direction on the next album. But I usually try to think as little as possible in those terms and more in terms of what would be good for the music we play, which will eventually determine the career anyway… I think it's (the music) the only thing that's got to matter in the end. On the rare occasions when we have over-concerned ourselves with extra-musical considerations, I think we've taken a little tumble. You know, when we've let ourselves be coerced or coerced ourselves into doing things just because they'd be good for our career. I've often found that because it's either destroyed something we've been trying to build up musically, or it's destroyed someone's confidence in you because you've gone against a couple of principles they admired you for, it's in actual fact not helped our career. So I like to think of the music, and everything we do going towards that, and our performance on stage, and try not to be involved in anything else. But I hate talking about "The Music" — it always sounds a bit false to me, especially when we've said over and over again that we're basically a rock and roll band, and a loud and fairly unsubtle one at that. I'd like to think we could be just accepted as that, and then if we do something that's a natural extension of that, but perhaps, a bit surprising...The thing is, I think, we'd like to stay within the structure of the band as it exists — which is a five piece rock band using organ, bass, guitar, drums and voice — and use it in any way possible to increase the ability of the group to entertain.... I think we've reached a lucky point in our lives where we can afford to take things at the right tempo, rather than that dreadful spurt we did after *Deep Purple In Rock* was big. We were working so hard then that the most simple argument could develop into 'I'm going to leave' with no trouble at all. Now I think we're a little slower coming to the boil."

In the same month that *Fireball* was released in the UK, Deep Purple were already working on material for the album that would come to be titled as *Machine Head*. Such material was already being used in the live shows. As was reported by the journalist, Richard Green, in *New Musical Express* in September 1971; "Little did the capacity crowd at Portsmouth Guildhall on Monday night know just how new Deep Purple's opening number 'Highway Star' really was. On the coach on the way down from London, Ian Gillan asked for suggestions for titles for a rock number. Roger Glover suggested 'Highway Star' and Ian set to writing it. It was finished during rehearsals and performed for the first time three hours later. It was the start of Purple's new British tour and if the audience reaction at Pompey is anything to go by, it'll be a stormer. A lot of venues are already sold out."

Hang on a minute? 'Highway Star' was written spontaneously on a tour bus? 'Highway Star'?! Yep! In *The Quietus*, Roger Glover was quoted as he elaborated on the matter in January 2011; "Yes, that is true. It was on a bus going down to Portsmouth and in those days to get a bit of publicity, we'd invite journalists to travel down with us. And there was a journalist called Richard Green who was known as The Beast. And I think he started talking about how songs get written. And songs were written in those days from jams. And I suppose it started out as a bit of a joke. Ritchie got a guitar and started playing and Ian started warbling about cars and I came up with the title, I was looking out of the window thinking, 'Well, here we are on the highway... Highway Star!' You know? And it just got thrown together and in fact I think we performed it that night, a sort

Machine Head Saves The Day

of embryonic version of it. Most great songs you hardly have to work on. 'Black Night' was another one. We were totally drunk and we'd given up. We were trying to write a single to please the management. We tried this and we tried that but finally we gave up and we went to the pub, went back and 'Black Night' almost appeared instantly. And we just wrote the stupidest words we could think of and it was a joke. And of course we thought it would never get used. Lo and behold it became one of our biggest hits. It's a lesson, really. You're at your best when you're not looking. Forget the head, you don't need the head. If you're thinking about it, it's a lost cause. It's got to come instinctively and spontaneously."

It was the same with 'Smoke On The Water'. Glover was quoted in the same feature; "Ritchie came out with the riff. We started jamming and it took us maybe all of two minutes to get an arrangement — 'Verse, punch-line, riff, verse, punch-line, riff, chorus, verse, out? Yeah, let's do that' — and then, of course, the circumstances under which that album was made were a little difficult. We had to move, it was recorded at some other place. But shortly after that we went to the Grand Hotel and started working on the other songs like 'Pictures Of Home'. And this first song we wrote we'd almost forgotten. And then I came up with the title, I used the words 'Smoke On The Water' but I didn't know what they meant at the time. And when we'd almost finished the album, we needed one more track. So we went, 'What about that track we did at that different place, let's have a look at that. And it's called 'Smoke On The Water' and it's about what happened to us here' so it was an afterthought in a way. And the words got written very quickly. They're almost conversational. No attempt to make them poetic or make them rhyme cleverly or anything like that. Not a lot of thought went into it."

Ritchie Blackmore recalled the ease with which 'Black Night' was written in an interview with Neil Jeffries in 1995; "That's a very nice memory. We went down the pub in Holborn. The management came in — it was the like Leggy Mountbatten thing from The Rutles — 'Lads! You need a hit!' — We were drinking, so we went back. I knocked out the Ricky Nelson 'Summertime' bass riff, which we did as a shuffle. We just added a couple of bits that worked very well. And all of a sudden it was number two."

Deep Purple - Fireball: In-depth

Glover recalled; "We were doing gigs at the time and it wasn't like now where you go in the studio and do an album. In those days you go and do a couple of days in the studio and then go out on the road for a couple of days and mix and match all the time. And that's kind of good in a way 'cause it keeps you fresh, and I think that's what makes *In Rock* such an uncompromising album."

Creative spontaneity continued successfully into the making of *Machine Head*. Roger Glover was quoted in *OnMilwaukee* in October 2019; "We had no idea at the time that we were creating something with such lasting appeal. I almost hate to admit it, but we wrote 'Smoke On The Water' as a filler track. We just made up some words about something that happened to us in Switzerland. That's not the sort of thing one expects to become a classic. I'd have to say the reason for the song's longevity is the riff. Ritchie just plucked it out of the air one day. It's so simple yet it's got an underlying complexity that's incredibly powerful."

Wait a moment! There I am going on about how *Fireball* was a rushed job and that there was no real amount of time blocked out in which the band could write songs for the album and yet, it didn't seem to be a creative barrier for Deep Purple when it came to how 'Black Night', 'Highway Star' and 'Smoke On The Water' were conceived; if some of Deep Purple's most iconic songs had come about as the result of spontaneity then what was really the problem with *Fireball*? Surely the same conditions were in place regarding being on the road a lot and having to write to a deadline to appease management. It could be down to a number of reasons; the nature of spontaneity, the power of hindsight, pot luck. It's hard to tell really because it's so flipping subjective in all fairness. Blackmore was quoted in *Melody Maker* in May 1972 as he admitted that the band hadn't really had much time to do proper rehearsals for *Machine Head*; "We haven't had time. If we are going to play anything new we usually make it up in the hotel before going on stage. We are doing three tracks off the new album, but we've been so busy we haven't had any time to rehearse the rest."

The problem of being overworked wasn't exclusive to when *Fireball* was being made and promoted. It is something that continued well into the days of making *Machine Head*. Ian Gillan later recalled;

Machine Head Saves The Day

"From the management's point of view there were no other major acts on their books, so on the one hand we couldn't complain that we were without their undivided attention, but then on the other hand we were being worked like dogs. I don't think any of us were well as arrangements were put in place to tour America yet again and make a new album in Montreux."

On reflection, it is pretty much the case that Gillan wasn't suddenly struck down with hepatitis, far from it! The symptoms had been there for a while, it's just that at the time, he had put them down to general stress and having been drinking a lot, it wasn't until he became alarmingly unwell whilst waiting for his bags in an airport that things began moving quickly and after being taken to Bethesda hospital in Chicago, a doctor told him that he was dangerously ill with hepatitis. Once he had come to, it was only after a total of five days in hospital that Gillan insisted that he was going to go home to England. The cancelled tour that resulted in this cost Deep Purple something to the tune of $200,000. Deep Purple definitely seem like a band who were being chronically overworked in the days that spanned the promoting of *Fireball* and the writing of *Machine Head*.

Gillan also recalled an occasion where Ritchie Blackmore didn't arrive for a rendezvous at a hotel reception one morning. It turned out that road manager Colin Hart, despite waking Blackmore up in time for the day, had found him in floods of tears in the corridor. I wonder if the haphazard nature with which some of the tour dates and locations were organised added undue stress to Deep Purple during the time of promoting *Fireball* as their most recent album.

As was reported in October 1971 in *New Musical Express*, "Deep Purple and Fleetwood Mac are to undertake twenty-one concert dates together during a four week tour of Canada this autumn. The itinerary opens at New York Madison Square Garden on October 22 and concludes in Bangor, Maine on November 21."

It seems that travel arrangements certainly had considerable moments of being dangerously below par too. Between the 17th and 18th June 1971, Deep Purple flew to Iceland to perform a one-off show in Reykjavik. The pilot of the hired plane had apparently only just got his license. Either way, he was less than professional. On the journey, during a bout of turbulence, the whole ceiling of the plane

Deep Purple - Fireball: In-depth

fell in. It exposed wiring. Plane staff were trying to push the wiring to the back of the plane despite there being smoke and flashing lights everywhere. The band yelled at them to stop it. Whilst the plane and everyone on it landed safely, the band refused to go home in it and reasonably so, insisted on another service for the return journey.

Ian Paice made a really interesting point about how in terms of how *Fireball* was received by listeners, it just didn't manage to strike a chord with people with the way that *In Rock* had. Paice advocated; "Fireball was lots of fun but it was a little more introvert, and there were some great tracks on it but it didn't fire up the imagination of the public in the way that *In Rock* did."

It does seem that compared to *Fireball*, more resources were invested in *In Rock* in some ways. Ritchie Blackmore was quoted in *Record Mirror* in May 1971; "The success of *In Rock* was largely due to the amount of time and effort we put into it. We worked for eight months on that album and it cost almost £10,000 in recording costs. Most groups only spend three months on average but the result is always three or four good tracks and the rest are mediocre, makeshift material made up in the studio to pad out the album and just get it out."

Having said that though, *Fireball* was in the pipeline for quite a long time after *In Rock* and it wasn't long after *Fireball* that the wheels were in motion for *Machine Head*. Even when *Fireball* was Deep Purple's most recent album to date, material that was due to be recorded for the *Machine Head* album featured strongly in the band's live sets. Of the song, 'Highway Star', Roger Glover was quoted in September 1971 in *New Musical Express*; "That came off very well. I'm looking forward to recording that, we'll be doing it on the next album which, incidentally will be out a lot sooner than this one (*Fireball*) was after *In Rock*."

In *Rolling Stone* in May 1972, Lester Bangs seemed to advocate that really, the beginning of things for Deep Purple happened with *In Rock* and that *Machine Head* was succeeding to carry the pace; "Their last three albums have finally found a comfortably furious groove for them to work in, making them prime contenders among the most searingly (sic) loud and heavy bands on both sides of the Atlantic. *Deep Purple In Rock* was a dynamic, frenzied piece of work sounding not a little like the MC5 (anybody who thinks that

Machine Head Saves The Day

all heavy bands put out thudding slabs of "downer" music just hasn't gotten into Deep Purple). *Fireball* was more of the same, if not quite as frantically effective. *Machine Head* bears strong similarities to both its immediate predecessors, lying qualitatively somewhere in between the two. And like both of them, though it delivers the sound, the rushing, grating crunch of the hard attack, it has its ups and downs compositionally. 'Highway Star' is a great opening track, quite similar both structurally and thematically to 'Speed King' and 'Fireball', the openers of the two previous albums. The pace is blistering, almost too fast for comfort, with lyrics that take the primeval cargirl equation and turn it into something as breathtakingly homicidal as Alice Cooper's 'Under My Wheels'."

In the same feature, Bangs continued to offer his opinion on *Machine Head* whilst presenting *In Rock*, *Fireball* and indeed *Machine Head* as a worthwhile trilogy in Deep Purple's discography up to that point; " 'Space Truckin'' is just as good, a sci-fi boogie that's the perfect answer to all the Kantnerian pomposities and turns out to be the missing link between them and things like Wild Man Fischer's 'Rocket Rock' (lyrically) and the Doors' 'Hello I Love You' (musically). Once again the lyrics are ace, and never let it be said that Deep Purple don't have a sense of humour. In between those two Deep Purple classics lies nothing but good, hard, socking music, although some of the lyrics may leave a bit to be desired. It says on the liner that 'This album was written and recorded in Montreux, Switzerland, between 6th and 21st December, 1971' and much of it sounds like it was conceived on the fly. There (were) even trials getting *Machine Head* recorded: it seemed that some local arsonist burned down the best recording studio in town but luckily the Rolling Stones' mobile unit was on hand to get the new D. Purple out on schedule... Now, I can't be that much of a purist, because I'm sure that 'Highway Star' and 'Space Truckin'' took at least twenty minutes each to compose, but I do know that this very banality is half the fun of rock 'n' roll. And I am confident that I will love the next five Deep Purple albums madly so long as they sound exactly like these last three."

It seems that for Deep Purple and many of their fans, *Machine Head* signified the band going back to the remit that it had set out with *In Rock* and thus, I would suggest that *Machine Head* is often spoken

Deep Purple - Fireball: In-depth

of as being superior to *Fireball*. However, *Fireball* is not without its merits and it is certainly the case that the making of *Machine Head* was not seamless either. As Pete Makowski put it in *Sounds* in March 1976; "('Smoke On The Water') tells the true story of the great casino disaster which occurred when the band went to Switzerland to record *Machine Head*. Apart from being a pretty slick crap joint, the casino was also a highly respected European venue and was going to be the location the band were going to record utilising a mobile unit. I say *were* because just before they got there disaster struck. It was on the night that Uncle Frank and The Mothers were playing there that, as the Purps put it: 'some stupid with a flare gun burnt the place to the ground'. Purple ended up recording the album at the Grand Hotel. The casino had to be completely rebuilt. Montreux is essentially a retiring home for rich persons. Like Brighton only a bit classier. It's a place where a millionaire can spend his last years in the healthiest of surroundings before pushing off to that great Swiss deposit account in the sky."

Sure, lessons were learnt from *Fireball* about what was needed to be carried forward (and indeed not) for the next album but equally, the pressure to make another album and the challenges of doing so whilst on the road were certainly not exclusive to *Fireball*.

Roger Glover said in *New Musical Express* in February 1972; "Ian's illness, hepatitis, was complicated with jaundice. His only cure is rest. We laid off for four or five weeks, and now Ian's got to take it very carefully. He can't lift anything now — not even a suitcase. But as long as he gets rest, he'll be fine. Apart from that the band is very happy together. We never even considered getting another singer in — no one suggested that. Mind you, a few people outside the band suggested we do some gigs without him. As it was, they almost had to force us on stage in Chicago without him. I think the rest period was very important, in that when you rest you think much more clearly. The resulting album, *Machine Head*, was one hundred per cent better as a result. We chose Switzerland to record the album simply for business reasons. It wasn't cheaper, or anything like that. We hired the Stone's mobile, and that isn't cheap. And by the time you add up things, like hotel bills, it works out pretty expensive. I'd hazard a guess at £8,000 — as compared to the last one, which cost

Machine Head Saves The Day

around the £6,000 mark. Getting the Stones' mobile was our idea — we'd heard it was a good one, and it cost us around £5,000 for the time we had it. We recorded the tracks from December 6th to 21st, working at least twelve hours a day, and the whole thing was mixed in three days. You know, it's a bit sick how people spend thousands and thousands of pounds building a recording studio, when we got the right sound in the corridor of a hotel. We hired a whole floor of the place and had mattresses up in the windows to avoid people outside from complaining about the sound. When we make an album we've got to be happy and relaxed, and if you've got hassles of getting equipment in from a rehearsal room, it doesn't help. It's worth the extra money we spend in studio time, just to be able to avoid the hassles."

It seems that Glover's optimism regarding *Machine Head* wasn't misplaced. In October 1972 in *New Musical Express* he said; "We've had a lot of bad luck with illness in the past. Ian Gillan was ill when *Fireball* was making it and Ritchie Blackmore was ill when *Machine Head* was taking off. Possibly that stunted their climb up the charts a little bit but *Machine Head* is now just about Gold, which is fantastic. It's the breakthrough we've been waiting for. The last couple of tours have proved we're making it on the concert scene. We're headlining and playing to capacity crowds. It really is a very good scene for us now. When Ian (Gillan) and I joined, the situation was that the band meant nothing here (UK) and were dwindling in America after a couple of hit singles, so we decided to concentrate on Europe, starting with the concerto, then *In Rock* and 'Black Night'. It happened for us and we were huge in Europe and meant nothing in America. The situation had been reversed. In the States, it's only now that we're getting over the 'Hush' thing, we still get people asking for it. 'Hush' isn't really what we want to be remembered for. It's the now band, the *Machine Head* band, that's the important one for us. At the moment we're in a satisfying position because we're fairly big in Europe and the States. That doesn't stop you trying to get bigger, of course."

As was reported in *Rolling Stone* in June 1973; "*Machine Head* was the one that broke open the US market, and back came Purple again for another try at an American tour. This time they lasted four days until Blackmore came down with hepatitis and flew home. Attempting to complete the tour with Al Kooper as a temporary stand-in, things went well during a hasty pre-show rehearsal. Shortly before showtime, however, Kooper had a nervous breakdown and cancelled out. Randy California was the next to step in and fill the vacant guitar spot in time for a Quebec show. Just prior to the group's boarding the plane to deliver them to the show, Air Canada went on strike... The band finally took off for their first major American tour in 1971. But then Gillan fell ill with hepatitis, and they went back to England and eventually to France (sic) to try and cut another album, renting out the empty, acoustically perfect Montreux ballroom. But two days before recording was to begin, the ballroom burned down."

Jon Lord was quoted in the same article; "We got diverted to the local theatre but that started shaking to pieces with the volume. The people who lived in the neighbourhood kept calling the cops. Finally we found a hotel that had been shut for the season. We soundproofed all the windows, sealed off one hall and made *Machine Head* in the corridor." There were certainly many obstacles to be overcome during the making of both *Fireball* and *Machine Head*.

Jon Lord told *Sounds* in April 1972; "I think we've always been a little scared of losing what we gained with *Deep Purple In Rock*, because each individual in the band had spent so long trying to achieve something, that when you eventually get there, half of you is saying you should perhaps move on from there, while the other half is saying 'don't knock a good thing' — I've seen it happen to so many bands — the first successful thing that happens to them tends to re-write their career for them for the next year or so."

In such regard, maybe the success of *In Rock* was pretty much as much of a blessing as it was a curse. Commercially, there is absolutely no denying what it did for Deep Purple but creatively, the pressure to live up to that kind of success could have certainly been a key ingredient that made *Fireball* higher pressured and a less enjoyable project in comparison. Some might even go as far as to say that post *Fireball*, *Machine Head* really saved Deep Purple's bacon and that, were it not for *Machine Head*, I could be telling a very different story right now.

I'm really not knocking *Fireball*. I promise I'm not, that's not the purpose of this book and it's not my job to do so. The fact is though that certainly, Ritchie Blackmore and Jon Lord seemed to both be

Machine Head Saves The Day

hoping that *Machine Head* would be many things that *Fireball* wasn't. Blackmore was quoted in *Disc & Music Echo* in March 1972; "I'm personally nearly always dissatisfied with what I've done, but this album (*Machine Head*) is pretty good. *In Rock* wasn't bad, but *Fireball* I wasn't happy with at all. I never play it, I hate it, we had no time and everything was made up in the studio. We found we got a much better sound with the mobile unit (for *Machine Head*) and the change of environment did us good too. The unit is just a lorry converted for recording and the sound you get at first is quite bad, which is clever because it makes you work for a better sound and when you come back and hear it on an English studio it's so much better because you've worked so much more to get the sound."

Blackmore said in May 1972 in *Melody Maker* on how he felt the fans were responding to Deep Purple at the time; "They are getting to know us well and the LPs are selling too. We seem to be the underground group for some reason, but we're getting the market together. This time we're only going there for two weeks to play the places we missed again, but we have two more American tours this summer."

At the time of the *Melody Maker* interview in May 1972, *Machine Head* was at number two in the British chart. Blackmore was quoted; "I think *Machine Head* is a good LP. Two tracks especially — 'Highway Star' and 'Smoke On The Water' — I like. The whole album is a lot better than the last one. *Fireball* was nothing really, but it depends on what you like."

Blackmore was quoted as he commented on what he considered to be the problem with *Fireball*; "I think the ideas are better and the group were playing well when we recorded it (*Machine Head*). The songs are more interesting too. We wrote when Ian (Gillan) was sick last time and we had a month off — it's the only time we get time off in this band when someone is ill. *Fireball* was written on tour which is a hopeless way of doing it."

When it came to picking a single from *Machine Head*, the band considered that the track, 'Never Before' would be the best option. It was the record company who insisted on 'Smoke On The Water'. It could just come down to a difference of opinion but also, maybe there's more in it as in, what the band overall considered would be

Deep Purple - Fireball: In-depth

commercially a good idea was not necessarily the same as what their record company had in mind. Imagine if 'Smoke On The Water' hadn't been released as a single! Even people who don't know any other Deep Purple songs are likely to know that one. I actually think that this is relevant to what happened with *Fireball* whereby what Deep Purple had in mind for the album may have been very different to the lines along which their record company were thinking. Such disparity could have had an impact on how *Fireball* was marketed. Such disparity could also explain why the band may have been disappointed that *Fireball* didn't live up to their initial expectations. I'm not saying that this was definitely the case, I'm just throwing out some theories here based on things that happened.

Machine Head was reviewed in *Cashbox* in April 1972; "When speaking of hard rock, one must speak of Deep Purple in the same breath. For they are forerunners in that category. After three albums with a now defunct label, and two with their current Warner Bros. affiliates, Deep Purple broke through with *Fireball*, their first effort to achieve national acclaim. Now, we are introduced to *Machine Head*, an album title that fully describes the power of the music contained within. The seven tracks in the set are all structured to display each member's individual talents — both as writers and musicians. *Machine Head* will be the album to throw the spotlight on a group that has long deserved its share of stardom."

As much as Ian Gillan spoke favourably of *Fireball*, he said of *Machine Head*; "As for *Machine Head*, it must have justified every single penny put into the new Purple label. We had made it with about two weeks' notice and although I was still in recovery (from hepatitis), it was our biggest album with classics like 'Highway Star', 'Space Truckin'', 'Never Before', 'Smoke On The Water', 'Maybe I'm A Leo', 'Lazy' and 'Pictures Of Home'. It sold three million copies quite quickly, made Deep Purple one of the biggest selling bands in the world and, with so much of our work, it has been selling year in, year out."

Glover said in February 1972 in *New Musical Express*; "The feeling in the group is that *Machine Head* is the best album we've ever made. When you look back, *Deep Purple In Rock* was a good album that said everything we wanted to say — it also had a lot of

Machine Head Saves The Day

fire. *Fireball*, was made in between tours. We didn't have a month off before, like we had with this album, and at times we'd be sitting in the studio desperate for ideas. The end result was technically better than *In Rock*, but it didn't have that inner spark. *Machine Head* is technically one step further than *Fireball*, plus it has that inner spark. I don't know how long we'll go on for, but speaking personally I couldn't be happier in the band than I am now. We still enjoy playing — and when we go on tour, the most enjoyable thing is the actual playing on stage. Sure we drink, and go to clubs and bars, but we try not to drink too much before we go on stage. You've got to look after yourself. We always have one drink before we go out there, just to loosen us up and take any worries away we may have. But heavy drinking — if at all — is done on a night off in a club."

I want to make it really clear here that many people, both members of Deep Purple and fans, often talk about *Machine Head* as if it is musically superior to *Fireball*. Whilst I've touched upon the concept in this chapter, it feels imperative to stipulate that it is not definitively the case that *Machine Head* is the better album of the two. Musically, they are both of merit, it's just that commercially, they meant very different things for Deep Purple as in, *Fireball* seems to have a reputation that is (sadly perhaps) tarred with problems whilst *Machine Head* often seems to be regarded as the turning point. Truthfully, *Machine Head* did well in the charts, Deep Purple seemed pleased with it, the songs from the album have been tremendously prominent in live sets to this day ('Highway Star' and 'Smoke On The Water' in particular!) and ultimately, *Machine Head* signified Deep Purple getting the audience engagement that they wanted from both America and Europe — it was the first of their albums to inspire audience interest from both markets at the time it was released. So of course, there are many robust reasons as to why it could be considered that for a band disillusioned with how *Fireball* performed, *Machine Head* did, in some ways save the day. However, and this is a huge however, I don't think it is fair to negate the merits of *Fireball* on the basis of what *Machine Head* achieved in comparison. As with *In Rock*, *Machine Head* was exceptional — just because *Fireball* wasn't commercially exceptional, it certainly doesn't mean that it wasn't worthwhile.

Chapter Eight
Fireball Is A Worthwhile Album

Overall, some of Deep Purple have been very critical of *Fireball*. In particular, Ritchie Blackmore came across as having been very disillusioned about the pressures that were put on the band by their management to make an album so promptly. In an interview with ABC Australia (I'm pretty sure that it was in the 1970s, possibly during the Rainbow years but it's a tough one to source admittedly), Blackmore said; "*Fireball*, that was a bit of a disaster 'cause it was thrown together in a studio. We had no time, managerial pressure; you've gotta play here, there, there, there, and you've gotta make an LP, then you're back in Australia then back to here. I got kind of bitter about that, I thought, if you want an LP you've gotta give us time, and they wouldn't, so I got a little bit bitter there and I just threw ideas to the rest of the group that I thought up on the spur of the moment. I had nothing in my head."

In an interview with music journalist, Steve Rosen, in 1974, Blackmore said; "The only one I haven't liked has been *Fireball*, that's the only one I thought was like, nowhere, yet I know a lot of people like that LP for some reason. I didn't see it, there's just nothing on it."

It seems that over time, Blackmore has pretty much stuck with his feelings of dissatisfaction towards *Fireball*. In September 1995 he told Neil Jeffries; "*Machine Head* is my favourite LP with Purple. It came after *Fireball*, which I thought was a complete flop, disastrous. There was just nothing on it worth talking about. I can't even remember any of the songs."

After some prompting from the interviewer, Blackmore added, "'Demon's Eye' was like a riff, 'Farmer's Daughter' ('Anyone's Daughter'!) was a spoof on country and western, 'No No No', to me,

Deep Purple - Fireball: In-depth

was bordering on banal. People liked the track, 'Fireball', but that was just fast with a double bass drum and an air-conditioning unit."

Although there was a lot of turbulence and frustrations during the making of *Fireball* that ultimately, resulted in it not being a favourite of most members of Deep Purple, the album really does have a lot going for it. It scored some fantastic reviews. *Fireball* was reviewed in September 1971 in *Record Mirror*; "Deep Purple have been very careful in bringing out this latest album. Some would say it's long overdue after the phenomenal success of *In Rock* but rather this is a beautifully timed release, coming at just the right moment. Purple play hard 'n' heavy, a mode of approach which demands that every song reaches a spectacular commercial standard. Heavy music, in fact, is perhaps the most commercial sound of the moment and, knowing this, Purple make sure they don't oversell themselves by limiting albums and singles to the absolute minimum. *Fireball* is an album much in the tradition of *In Rock* but you'll find more variety in there this time. There's no questioning every member of Purple's instrumental ability and on a country flavoured song called 'Anyone's Daughter' vocalist, Ian Gillan, shows that removed from his usually more hysterical role, has a good voice in the best ballad tradition. None of the material is particularly "great", it doesn't bear comparison to material by John/Taupin or Taylor or Young, but then it's not meant to. Deep Purple do what they do with taste and discretion. In fact, probably better than any comparable act in the world."

I'm very cautious that it is sometimes stated that overall Deep Purple didn't like *Fireball* because, Deep Purple (as it was at the time) consisted of five strong minded individuals, each with their own opinions. In an interview with music journalist, Steve Rosen, in 1974, Ian Gillan said; "I always had this big debate with Ritchie and Jon and little Ian and Rog about my favourite Purple album, and I'll tell you the reason why in a second. My favourite Purple album was *Fireball*, and the reason I like that so much is because I felt it was, from a writing point of view, it was really the beginning of tremendous possibilities of expression. I just went out and bought it yesterday again in New York and some of the tracks on that album, I think are really, really effective. In those days, before it was really

Fireball Is A Worthwhile Album

being called heavy rock, it was still being called rock, progressive rock, or something like that, which was the tag that was being put onto it, that kind of music, and I really thought that some of the tracks on there were very progressive rock numbers, very progressive. And I've been playing it again now. I listen to *In Rock*, which I'm knocked out with, but I thought it was a shame that we didn't continue with that sort of expression in our writing, as opposed to the slightly formulated approach to our later albums."

I actually think that Ian Gillan's perspective on *Fireball* is mind blowing as in, it encouraged me to think of the album very differently, very differently indeed as in, a lot of the rest of Deep Purple's complaint with *Fireball* seems to be in terms of how it compared to *In Rock* and eventually *Machine Head*; call it the *In Rock* yardstick if you will. Now then, by changing this yardstick to prog rock as in "how does *Fireball* fare as a progrock album?", then all of a sudden there's a very different way of looking at *Fireball* than say, comparing it to *In Rock*; by saying that *In Rock* is definitive of the Deep Purple sound and that *Fireball* is less worthy because it deviates from that, well, it ultimately writes *Fireball* off rather than encouraging people to embrace and indeed enjoy it in its own right.

Take some of the more structurally free and if you will, meandering tracks on *Fireball* and if you compare them to the tighter structure of the songs on *In Rock* then *Fireball* feels like it's a bit lost at sea. However, accept *Fireball* as something that is more in the lexicon of prog rock and all of a sudden, a lot of what is going on, on that album feels justified and no longer the poorer sibling to *In Rock*.

Admittedly, I for one am actually very grateful for Ian Gillan's perspective on *Fireball* because it made me look at it in a different way (not that I disliked it anyway!). I hope that even just one person reading this might get something similar from Gillan's thoughts on *Fireball* as in, change the yardstick by which you measure it against and then bam! The quality of the album really comes into its own.

Gillan was quoted in *New Musical Express* in March 1971; "The tracks (on *Fireball*) would have been out of place on *In Rock* but they seem to be a natural extension, The only common ingredient in both albums is earthiness."

Ian Gillan said of *Fireball* in his 1998 autobiography; "Opinions

Deep Purple - Fireball: In-depth

varied about *Fireball* and I know Ritchie was quoted as saying 'it was nothing, really' — he went on to (helpfully) add that being on tour was no way to write an album. In fact, he said the only time we got to write in Deep Purple was when someone was ill. Given that during this period most of us had been ill, including himself with appendicitis, I'm surprised he didn't feel better about the project. As for me, I thought we kept up our progressive standards with the album, and am proud of it. Songs like 'No No No', 'Demon's Eye', 'The Mule', 'Fools', 'Anyone's Daughter' and 'No One Came' — well, those songs are fine by me! However, if I liked the album, I was definitely in the minority because Jon, Roger and Ian Paice were pretty negative about it as well. Still, it can't have been that bad because it went to the top of the UK charts in September and made number thirty-two in the States in July 1971."

Whilst some advocate that *Fireball* was less rock orientated than *In Rock*, others complained that it was still too loud. You can't please all of the people all of the time! Besides, I get the impression that the following reviewer wasn't a fan of rock music on a general basis. *Fireball* was reviewed in an American paper in August 1971. I'm sorry to say that I sourced this from a stray newspaper clipping where the information on what paper it actually was had been cut off (such is the nature of this kind of research!). A worthwhile review though and thus it is as follows; "Deep Purple, the English rock group that had a huge hit with 'Hush' in the US several years ago, has retrenched itself after a reorganizational shuffle. The band is hard and more introspective, heavier and louder than its original sound which flowed instead of roared. The five-man group, which suffered an immense setback when its American recording firm, Tetragrammaton, folded after a year of operation, is now attempting to re-establish itself in America as a contending rock group. The album should blow the minds of hard rock fans, but it won't do much to spread the group's name among the softer rock fans, for there is little soft about the album. The title tune is a real ripper which has potential, 'Strange Kind Of Woman' has been a hit in England and 'Anyone's Daughter' is a pure country rocker which is the best on the album. The group shows it has the ability to play softly — and play exceedingly well — in the moody 'Fools', its talent in this direction

Fireball Is A Worthwhile Album

should be exploited, for its potential along these lines appears superb. But the group's main thrust is loud and hard, and that is something almost any group can do with a fair amount of success. But it takes a polished group to play quietly and gain respect. Deep Purple has the talent to quiet its tones and retain the respect it has earned as a rock group. It will probably gain more respect if it has the guts to quiet (sic) down. Three out of five stars."

A number of songs from the *Fireball* album seemed to be put to good use in the band's live performances. Deep Purple's performance at The Purley Orchid Ballroom in England was reviewed in *New Musical Express* in February 1972; "Forget about chart placing and record sales for just one moment. The true testing point of any big group is its drawing capacity at the box office, and from what I saw on Tuesday it would appear that Deep Purple are enjoying the very best of both worlds. On a night which should have kept most people at home and in front of the fire, Purple attracted well over 3,000 exuberant devotees for the grand opening of the Orchid Ballroom's season of heavy rock attractions. When groups reach the status that Purple now find themselves with — acclaimed on both sides of the Atlantic — they do one of two things; become complacent and predictable or they improve. Deep Purple have not only improved since the last time I witnessed their high-energy performance at Royal Albert's emporium, but they've also become a whole lot funkier. Familiar favourites like 'Strange Kind Of Woman', 'Child In Time', 'Fireball' and 'Speed King' have been slightly re-worked to accommodate the new funkier approach, and from the ecstatic reaction from the crowd it would appear that there's still considerable mileage left in Deep Purple's brand of cerebral rock."

Journalist, Richard Green, described the live performances of some of the songs from *Fireball* in September 1971 in *New Musical Express*; "The revamped 'Strange Kind Of Woman' is a lot cleaner. Ritchie's solo in particular being more defined and clear cut. 'No No No' from the album got the reception it deserved, being heavy and forceful. Ritchie excelled yet again and Ian Gillan had a good time with his maracas which always seem to egg on the audience."

In the same feature, Roger Glover was quoted as he added; "I enjoyed it because it's a stompy kind of thing. We run the risk of doing all our numbers too fast, it's good to slow it down sometimes. Perhaps it was a bit too fast."

Of course, classics from the *In Rock* album were a staple part of the set too. As Richard Green continued in the same feature; "My old favourite, 'Child In Time' had Jon Lord and Ian Paice really getting together for a swinging jazz passage which Jon and Ritchie transformed into a rock session. Ian Gillan brought his congas on to add to the overall sound." Also, at the particular show that was reviewed, 'Speed King' was played as part of the encore.

It's plausible that Deep Purple's preference for playing live rather than in a studio may come to the fore here as in, the studio version of any given track from *Fireball* may have fared better (at least in Ritchie Blackmore's opinion) live. In an interview with Steve Rosen in 1974, Blackmore said; "On stage you have a lot of intense excitement. It's like adrenalin of nervous presence. People I know love it or they get scared of it."

This preference for playing live rather than in the studio seems to have been a longstanding thing for Blackmore. In another interview with Steve Rosen, in 1978, he said; "To get it onto tape, is a pain in the fucking arse. I don't like recording too much, It's too clinical. A lot of people love it 'cause they can edit their music and make it nice but when they get on stage they're lost. My type of thinking is the opposite, I love to have that freedom, just going on stage and playing whatever I want to play at the time. I'll play the numbers which I'm supposed to play but the in between parts, when I'm feeling good, I'll be away and play something completely off the wall that I've never ever played in my life."

Even whilst *Fireball* was still being made, Ian Gillan advocated of enjoying the artistic freedom that came with playing live. He was quoted in *New Musical Express* in March 1971 as he offered some insight into the live shows; "Nothing is worked out. If something happens and gets a good reaction you may do it again three nights later subconsciously, then you may do it three months later."

There is certainly a lot to be said for the innovation present on *Fireball* as a studio album though, both in and of itself on that particular album as well as recording techniques that would be used in later albums. You certainly can't say that there was no creativity

Fireball Is A Worthwhile Album

when it came to recording *Fireball*. In the 1972 UK released *Machine Head* songbook (it's not an entire band score, it contains the sheet music for all songs on the album and even features 'Black Night' as a bonus. All scores are just chords, piano and vocal lines), Roger Glover wrote in an introductory feature at the beginning of the book; "Although we were aware of this some time ago, it really became apparent one day during the making of the *Fireball* album. Ian Paice was walking around carrying his snare drum and hitting it. As he walked from the studio area into the corridor on his way to the control room in the old De Lane Lea studios, Kingsway, he noticed the change in sound of his snare drum. It was so dramatic that he called us all in and demonstrated the difference between the quiet 'toc' of the drum in the soundproofed, padded and baffled studio, and the resounding crash of the drum in the corridor, bringing out the full range of sound... the real sound, exciting and loud! From that point to the end of the making of *Fireball*, Ian set his drums up in the corridor, greatly inconveniencing everybody, but getting such a good sound that we all forgave him."

Glover said in February 1972 in *New Musical Express*; "We're pretty polite to one another, although I admit that can be a bad thing. Bad in that if you have a grudge against someone else, you don't always come out with it. The only one I socialise with is Ian Paice, simply because we live together. Certainly we're the two best people in the group to live together, the bass player and drummer. More in sympathy with one another. I've learnt a lot from Ian. He's forever practising, and he'll play records of drummers and players that turn him on, and I'll buy records by people who turn me on. So we both hear all kinds of different music and musicians."

The first sound that meets the listener's ears on *Fireball* is the sound of an air conditioning unit being turned on. It had been recorded by assistant sound engineer, Mike Thorne, prior to Deep Purple requesting such sound effect. In the studio, Roger Glover suggested to Martin Birch that the sound of a machine starting up would be an interesting way to begin the song 'Fireball' as the opening and indeed title track on the album.

Birch was struggling to find a suitable sound effect but then Thorne suggested the recording that he had already made. At the time, Deep Purple claimed that the sound was made by a special synthesiser. The sound was actually made by numerous large tube mics being placed strategically in the studio's air conditioning closet. With added reverb and effective use of the control room, Thorne turned the air conditioning unit on and recorded the sound of it reaching full power. He then turned the air conditioning unit off which resulted in the recorded sound having the range of textures that it does. He filed the recording away in a box that he labelled the West Uzbekistan Percussion Ensemble. Perhaps that was due to him being in an assistant's role at De Lane Lea studios; maybe it would have looked a bit weird to file the recording that sat there forgotten about for a while under "air conditioning unit" or similar. Thorne's spontaneous innovation in the form of what came to be known by many as the "Fireball whoosh" sat unused in the studio until Glover put the idea out there that a sound effect would be a good start to 'Fireball'.

Unusually, the track 'Fireball' doesn't feature a lead guitar solo. Instead, Roger Glover plays a bass guitar solo that is followed by an organ solo from Jon Lord. It wasn't until the release of the 25th Anniversary edition of the album that a studio version of the song included a guitar solo by Ritchie Blackmore; on 'Fireball (Take 1 — Instrumental)' a bonus track on the album, Blackmore's guitar solo appears near the end of the song where, on the original LP, a fade out had been placed prior to that.

The version of 'Fireball' that was originally released was one of the few Deep Purple songs to feature Glover having more solo time than Blackmore. It is also one of the few Deep Purple songs that features Ian Paice using double bass drums. As was reported in *New Musical Express* in September 1971, Ian Paice had another bass drum brought in for playing 'Fireball' live in order to get the volume across in the context of the speed that the band played the song on stage. *Fireball* certainly showcased some fantastic drumming from Ian Paice.

In October 2014, journalist, Pete Kaufmann, advocated of 'Fireball' in *Modern Drummer*; "The musicality, power, and creativity of Paice's drumming is stamped all over Purple's catalogue. Take the opening title track of 1971's *Fireball*, whose blistering double

Fireball Is A Worthwhile Album

bass and syncopated bell and snare patterns during the intro come at you like a bull out of the gate. (It's actually a rare instance of Paice playing double bass. So rare, in fact, that he needed to grab a spare drum left in the studio — by the Who's Keith Moon!)."

The 'Fireball' single was reviewed in *Melody Maker* in October 1971; "Amazing drum solo from speed ace Ian Paice, leads into a driving and exciting cut from their album of the same name. A mite fast for a hit single but should shake a few juke boxes apart."

The innovation that was present on *Fireball* was certainly worthwhile, so much so that it had an influence on how *Machine Head* was to be recorded. Glover said; "*Machine Head* was a conscious effort by us to change the sound. Thinking about live sounds, we'd always preferred the sound of the band live, in a hall, in a theatre or whatever, and during the making of *Fireball*, we experimented with putting the drums in the corridor to get that sort of "slap-back" sound. Studios were always padded and they sounded really good for folk music but rock didn't seem right. So we took it one stage further, we decided to go and record the entire album with a mobile studio, in a theatre setting, without the audience, so it would be like a live album but with the luxury of being able to redo songs if we didn't like them. So we looked around and figured that we'd do it in Montreux, where the casino was a regular gig and any European tour, any self-respecting band would have played the casino 'cause it was part of the circuit."

Individuals wondering about life outside of Deep Purple was not something that was exclusive to the days of *Fireball*. Even a month after *Machine Head* had been released, ever the pragmatist, Jon Lord was quoted in April 1972 in *Sounds*; "You see the band still thoroughly enjoys playing on stage in front of an audience — there's not one member who doesn't feel that's still the best moment, so I think just from that point of view the band will probably stick together. A couple of us are at the point now where we probably wouldn't join another group if we left this one. But it all depends — it could last another three years, or it could last another three months; you never know when a group's at this stage. It's a happy unit and a successful one, so it could conceivably go on for a long time, but somebody might just get to the stage where they think they'd

Deep Purple - Fireball: In-depth

really rather be doing something else. And I don't think the group would continue if one person left — we've reached such a point of interdependence. I'd be able to tell you better if it happened, but I think we'd call it a day."

It really comes across that everyone in Deep Purple perhaps had a bit of a love/hate relationship with the whole thing at times, regardless of the album in question. Ritchie Blackmore said in *Disc & Music Echo* in March 1972; "I think in another year or so we'll say that's it, no more gigs. I find it like going into the army. You say goodbye to your friends — and tell them you hope you'll see them again. You eat hamburgers with no vegetables and once you've been in one Holiday Inn you've been in them all. Everybody comes up trying to lay drugs on you and says 'what are you on man?' and as they won't believe we're not on anything we usually tell them we're into canary droppings. But the audiences, for all that, are incredible, when you go on stage it's a great feeling of everyone waiting for you, and they really appreciate you."

Regardless of what anyone says about *Fireball*, good or bad, in the grand scheme of things, it was certainly part of a long term progression on the road to success. Glover said in February 1972 in *New Musical Express*; "As a group we're probably one of the best paid. For an English gig we get around £1,000, and although that sounds a lot, you've got to realise it costs us that a week just to run our business. The expenses are enormous. We all pay individually for our own instruments, and every six months we go and see our group accountant and he tells us how much money we have. We started off in the red — our management put £20,000 into the group, and it took us till the end of '70 for us to pay it off. My only thoughts are how incredibly lucky I am. I buy a lot of records, and I have good stereo equipment, but I haven't really spent that much money. If I'm in a restaurant somewhere, I always want to buy everyone I'm with a meal. The most expensive thing I've bought is my house in Iver, which I'm hoping to move into soon, Ian Paice is the only one who hasn't bought a house now — I think he's waiting for somewhere like Buckingham Palace. Obviously, money invested in a house is well spent, but apart from that I like to paint — not very often, just for a few days in bursts — so one of my bedrooms is going to be a

Fireball Is A Worthwhile Album

studio. A studio come darkroom actually, because I'm also interested in photography. I've recently bought a good camera. It's something I want to take up seriously. Whilst I was at school I made my decision to be an artist, and towards the latter end of my schooling, after two years at art college, I became pretty disillusioned. I gathered I couldn't become an artist simply because I was told I didn't have enough O Levels. As it was, I had to do a vocational course, and I started doing interior design. After a while I decided to sling it in favour of being in a group, but everyone else said I'd be an idiot to give it up. Whilst I was deciding. I had a nervous breakdown. I remember there was a woman teacher at college who helped me a lot by saying 'don't do what you think you ought to do — do what you want to do. Then if it turns out wrongly, you won't have any regrets' so I took her advice, and I've always gone by what she said then. I've learned that whatever happens, whatever I do, regret never changes anything. I seem to have found happiness within myself. No matter what goes wrong, it never affects my happiness."

Ian Gillan advocated that the lyrics of 'Fireball' are about unrequited love. The single itself got to number fifteen in the UK charts. It is the first instance of Ian Paice playing a double bass drum. 'Fireball' was dropped from the band's set list not long after it was added. It is possible that this may be due to the fact that a second bass drum being required wasn't ergonomic at the time for live performances. It is considered by some that the use of the two kick drums in 'Fireball' functioned as an early inspiration for a technique that came to be used often in heavy metal music.

'No No No' is said to be a political and social protest song about environmental destruction. 'Anyone's Daughter' is arguably a classic Ian Gillan song in terms of how it tells a story. 'The Mule' features lyrics about Isaac Asimov's character from the *Foundation* series of books. Ian Gillan has said so on his website although also, on the *Live In Concert 1972/73* DVD, he introduces the song by saying; "It's all about Lucifer and some of his friends, most of whom are sitting around here somewhere tonight."

It's hard to tell which is true really as in, in many interviews of his with the media over the years, Gillan often came across as having a bit of an "anything for a laugh" approach to expressing himself. Mind

Deep Purple - Fireball: In-depth

you, the same can be said for Ritchie Blackmore (in a promotional video recording of 'Fireball' that took place in a TV studio, he held his guitar backwards in humorous defiance at having to mime to a backing track). That's rock stars for you I guess. Nevertheless, 'The Mule' is another excellent example of the originality that is present on *Fireball*, particularly in the context of the recording process.

As Roger Glover wrote in the liner notes for the 25th Anniversary edition of the album; "In an effort to achieve a phlanging effect the tape had been reversed and was in the "record" mode... Half the drums had been erased from the middle to the end of the song. The drums used for the recording had been packed and were on their way to Europe for the next tour dates. A kit was hastily rented and Ian had to overdub new drums onto half the song."

Overall, 'The Mule' is pretty much an iconic track for Deep Purple. It was recorded live for the *Made In Japan* album in August 1972 where it features one of the all-time greatest conversations where Gillan begins the song by saying the famous, "Alright... everything up here...please. And a bit more monitor if you've got it", to which Blackmore replied, "You want everything louder than everything else?" with Gillan confirming, "Yeah, can I have everything louder than everything else." Endearing really isn't it? As in, for all the arguments, friction and disagreements that may have been going on behind the scenes, as a live band, there was certainly a time where Blackmore and Gillan had a brilliant professional and musical rapport.

There is an extent of religious imagery in 'Fools'. In the 25th Anniversary edition of *Fireball*, Roger Glover wrote in the liner notes; "It's about a guy who dies and he's looking back and can see the world is run by fools. Ian's voice has 'thickened' on this one. We'd been using the guitar solo on stage for some time, we never thought it would work on record, but it's great. None of it was worked out, it's just adlibbed."

Also, Ritchie Blackmore used the same volume swells that he had been using when playing 'Mandrake Root' live. In Ian Gillan's book, *Child In Time*, he stipulated that 'No One Came' is representative of a fear he had that one day he would play a show and nobody would show up. Again, 'No One Came' is demonstrative of

Fireball Is A Worthwhile Album

the innovation that went on with the recording process. Glover wrote in the 25th Anniversary edition of the album's liner notes; "When we first recorded it, there seemed to be an awkward ending, so we made a "loop" of eight bars of the basic riff and edited it on to the end. Jon sat at the piano and played anything that came into his head while in the control room, on an empty piece of tape we recorded it, slowing it down and speeding up the tape speed, creating a strange effect. This was then reversed and overdubbed randomly on to the new end section. No one knew what it would sound like but the very first time we tried it we loved the placement of it and that became final position."

Essentially, all seven songs on *Fireball* (both the UK and US versions!) are worthwhile in terms of the fruitfulness that was present musically and in the recording studio. The same applies regarding the album's artwork. *Cash Box* reported in March 1972; "At a luncheon at the Savoy Hotel, the *New Musical Express* presented their 1972 awards. Instituted in 1968, the awards 'recognise the creative and technical achievements of the British record industry.' For the best designed LP sleeve in the Pop category, the award went to Castle Chappell for *Fireball* by Deep Purple."

As much as most of Deep Purple seem to have been underwhelmed with *Fireball* overall, it was certainly not a blip on the band's long-term legacy. Maybe it is with time that *Fireball* fared well in terms of popularity. Of course, that is a very subjective and immeasurable thing but all the same, when MkII reformed, *Fireball* was certainly marketed enthusiastically as part of their legacy by that time. As was reported in *Billboard* in February 1985; "To mark the reunion of the Deep Purple line-up of Blackmore, Gillan, Glover, Lord and Paice, and to link with the band's upcoming world tour, EMI is marketing three previous studio albums from the band, each in gatefold PVC sleeves and with posters of different individual Purple members. The albums, *Machine Head*, *Fireball* and *Deep Purple In Rock*, retail at roughly $6.20." Ian Gillan was quoted in *Kerrang!* in January 1987; "Without doubt it's (*House Of Blue Light*) my favourite album since *Fireball*."

In 1996 when the 25th Anniversary edition of *Fireball* was released, it came to light that some tracks that didn't make the final cut of the original album were absolute gold, well, I would argue that they are anyway. When I first heard 'Slow Train', I couldn't believe that something so good didn't get to see the light of day on the original release of *Fireball* at the time. The mind boggles. Everyone's mileage may vary in terms of the opinion that I hold on the song but really, there genuinely doesn't seem to be anything about it that isn't worthy. Glover wrote for the liner notes; "'Slow Train', the song that never made the album, had been written during the sessions in The Hermitage and, although a fair amount of work had gone into it, we obviously felt that it wasn't good enough for the album. The fact that it has remained unknown and unexploited until now is nothing short of miraculous, given that years later, dredging the archives for more and more unreleased "product" was a consuming passion for both management and record company. The other song, 'Freedom', has been remixed here and is a great example of the curious mix of rock 'n' roll and hard rock that is one of the band's traits."

Personally, it blows my mind that 'Slow Train' didn't make it to the original version of *Fireball*. It's a great song with all of the ingredients that make a good Deep Purple song; brilliant riff, sparkling vocals from Gillan and an overall memorable melody. It's a good thing that 'Slow Train' eventually saw the light of day, I think it would have been a real shame had it not (that said, Blackmore and Glover reprised part of 'Slow Train' years later on the Rainbow track, 'Make Your Move' — it features on their 1983 album, *Bent Out Of Shape*).

Glover also wrote for the liner notes; "With *Fireball*, for me at least, there was a sense of having to follow up a huge hit — something that was completely new to me. I believe we all felt the need to prove ourselves and *Fireball* seems to me now to be more of a considered album than the brasher and bolder *In Rock*. That it didn't subsequently do as well (except for the States where it made some headway, going Gold) was initially a disappointment, at least to me, but to suggest that it is an inferior album is to do it a disservice. It was a real progression for the band and an adventurous time when we were ready to explore the increasing possibilities of the studio."

It is possible that with hindsight, some members of Deep Purple may have looked back at *Fireball* years later with more fondness for

Fireball Is A Worthwhile Album

the album than they may have had at the time. There's a relatively recent interview with Jon Lord (easily post 2000) where he spoke at length regarding his thoughts on *Fireball*; "*Fireball* is a troublesome album because to me, you couldn't have had *Fireball* without *In Rock*, but you couldn't have had *Machine Head* without *Fireball* so it sits very nicely as part of those three really good rock albums, and I think the fact that it wanders slightly from the remit that we'd set up with *In Rock*, doesn't worry me at all. I love *Fireball*, I think it does good things. I think it goes to places that the band wasn't expected to go to. The title track, I love that thing. Ritchie loved playing fast, he loved challenging the rest of the band to play fast. Paicey's drumming is dramatically good on that track. The over amplified sound of an air conditioning unit being switched on at the beginning to replicate the sound of, I don't know, a spaceship taking off? I'm not quite sure what it was meant to be but it's pretty cool. I'm very fond of the organ solo on that. It was bloody difficult to play and I was very happy with it. I just think it's a great idea for a rock song. Good words, and a wonderful turnaround in the middle, lovely chord changes. I think the album, again, because of its various light and shade moments, surprised one or two real heavy rock fans. I think they thought perhaps it went a bit light in a couple of places, but I love it, it's great. There's a great song on it called 'No No No' which I think is fabulous. 'Fools', great song, great song. 'Anyone's Daughter' is great. It's a weird little sidestep, why not?"

That said, Ritchie Blackmore was quoted in *The Guardian* in April 2015; "My favourite LP would be *Machine Head* followed closely by *In Rock* and then *Burn*. *Fireball* I didn't like." Oh well, there's no pleasing everyone. Besides, one of the best things about Deep Purple MkII is that creatively, it consisted of five strong minded individuals, all of whom brought something to the table and thus, it is inevitable that *Fireball* divided opinion, even among Deep Purple themselves.

There is no denying that *Fireball* was a success on the basis that it reached number one in the UK and a respectable number thirty-two in the US. Sure, it was not in the charts for as long as *In Rock* was but I think it's really important to stipulate here that *In Rock* was pretty exceptional in that regard anyway. It seems quite futile to consider

Deep Purple - Fireball: In-depth

that *Fireball* was inferior to *In Rock* when actually, the success of *In Rock* was to an extent that it moved the goalposts so significantly anyway; *Fireball* in and of its own right did worthwhile things as an album.

'Strange Kind Of Woman' has been a staple of Deep Purple's live sets right into the present day and 'Fireball' has often been used in encores over the years. Ian Gillan told *New Musical Express* in September 1971; "We're only keeping two of the old numbers, putting in three from the new album (*Fireball*) and two completely new numbers (that would come to be recorded for *Machine Head* — 'Highway Star' and 'Lazy'). 'Strange Kind Of Woman' developed into a very good number in America so we're keeping that but we're dropping things like 'Wring That Neck', 'Black Night' and 'Speed King' and now we're just keeping our fingers crossed. I've got butterflies. I always do before a new tour starts."

As it happens, 'Speed King' was featured in the live set that the journalist doing the interview reviewed. Still though. In the same feature, Roger Glover was quoted as he gave his opinion on the song, 'Lazy'; "I really enjoyed doing that, that'll be on the next album as well."

'Strange Kind Of Woman' and 'The Mule' feature on the 1972 live album, *Made In Japan*; that very fact alone certainly conflicts with the argument that by 1972, it was all about *Machine Head* as in, even with the success of *Machine Head*, material from *Fireball* was still worthy of Deep Purple's live sets. The call and response between Gillan and Blackmore during 'Strange Kind Of Woman' on *Made In Japan* is an absolute treat to the ears (unless you don't like Gillan's high pitched screaming singing!). 'Anyone's Daughter' was played in live sets circa 1993-1994 whilst 'Fools', 'Demon's Eye', 'No No No', 'No One Came' and 'I'm Alone' have all been used sporadically in the band's live sets since 1996.

Glover was quoted in *OnMilwaukee* in October 2019; "The hardcore fans like to hear some of the more obscure cuts, but there are songs that we just can't leave out because a lot of people want to hear the stuff from *Machine Head* and *Fireball*. Those are the ones that have lasted."

It is a likelihood that most of the songs on *Fireball* might not

Fireball Is A Worthwhile Album

be known to someone who hasn't listened to the whole album due to the fact that they don't get a lot of airplay on most classic rock radio stations. There are definitely some hidden gems on the original *Fireball* LP and indeed the 25th Anniversary edition of the album released in 1996. Put the drama of the making of the album aside for a moment and the songs themselves feature plenty of it and beautifully so too.

'The Mule' seems to have some elements of psychedelic influences and 'Fools' goes from feeling pretty calm to building in tension prior to the breakout of a heavy riff. The order of the songs on the LP really have the potential to take the listener on a journey with them. After 'Fireball' grabs your attention, 'No No No' comes in with a bluesier feel to it where there's some great interplay between organ and guitar before the lively and memorable riff on 'Demon's Eye' kicks in (and on the US version, 'Strange Kind Of Woman' offers an equally interesting kind of groove as the third track).

Sure, 'Anyone's Daughter' is a quirky one as far as the typical Deep Purple sound goes but again, why not? You can't say that Deep Purple were afraid to experiment and 'Anyone's Daughter' is a good example of that. It feels suitably placed at the end of what side one of the LP has to offer. 'The Mule' is attention grabbing and a good start to side two of the LP. 'Fools' offers lots of interest on the riff, as do the groovy melodies of 'No One Came'. Again, some great soloing and call and response moments between Blackmore and Lord on that track.

Fireball is a classic Deep Purple album in its own right. Things may have been challenging for the band at the time of making and promoting the album but historically, it is very much an important part of Deep Purple's discography. Many may view it as the bridge between *In Rock* and *Machine Head* and in some ways, it does make sense that it is viewed in such a way when you look at what people's overall expectations may be in terms of the sound and kind of music they expect from Deep Purple, as was epitomised with *In Rock* in 1970.

Still though, embrace and welcome *Fireball* into your playlist as something that stands alone as a good album and certainly, it is entirely worth listening to. *In Rock* and *Machine Head* were two

Deep Purple - Fireball: In-depth

fantastic Deep Purple albums both musically and in terms for what they did for the band commercially. It is plausible that historically, *Fireball* is vulnerable to being an overshadowed album in Deep Purple's discography purely on the basis that is falls between those two particular albums chronologically. It would perhaps be an overstatement to say that *Fireball* is entirely underrated but equally it is plausible that it is prone to being overlooked compared to Deep Purple's other albums. I think it is important to acknowledge this because *Fireball* is a meaningful album in its own right and it would be a real shame for it to be negated by new listeners.

Personally, I see no reason as to why people won't be listening to Deep Purple in another fifty years' time. In fact, it's trippy to think that *Fireball* is fifty years old even now! There is something to be gained from every playing of that album. Musically, it has lots of "wow!" moments and to not give it a chance would certainly be a missed opportunity.

Appendices

Personnel

Deep Purple
Ian Gillan — lead vocals
Ritchie Blackmore — rhythm and lead guitars
Jon Lord — keyboards, Hammond organ
Roger Glover — bass guitar
Ian Paice — drums

Production
Recorded between September 1970 and June 1971 at De Lane Lea Studios, Olympic Studios, and The Hermitage
Engineered by Martin Birch, Lou Austin and Alan O'Duffy
Peter Mew — Original album remastering
Tom Bender — Engineering work on the bonus tracks

Cover design by Castle, Chappell and Partners Limited. Photography by Tarly Burrett, Chagford Studios.

Fireball Track Listings

Original LP, UK Version
A1. Fireball (3:21)
A2. No No No (6:40)
A3. Demon's Eye (5:19)
A4. Anyone's Daughter (4:29)
B1. The Mule (5:16)
B2. Fools (8:15)
B3. No One Came (6:25)

Original LP, US Version
A1. Fireball (3:21)
A2. No No No (6:40)
A3. Strange Kind of Woman (4:04)
A4. Anyone's Daughter (4:29)
B1. The Mule (5:16)
B2. Fools (8:15)
B3. No One Came (6:25)

25th Anniversary Edition, 1996
8. Strange Kind of Woman (a-side remix '96) (4:07)
9. I'm Alone (single b-side) (3:08)
10. Freedom (album out-take) (3:37)
11. Slow Train (album out-take) (5:38)
12. Demon's Eye (remix '96) (6:13)
13. The Noise Abatement Society Tapes (Midnight in Moscow, Robin Hood, William Tell) (4:17)
14. Fireball (take 1 — instrumental) (4:09)
15. Backwards Piano (Reversed piano solo at the end of No One Came) (0:56)
16. No One Came (remix 96) (6:24)

Discography

USA
Original July releases:
Warner Bros BS 2564, LP
Warner Bros M5 2564, cassette
Warner Bros WBM8 2564, 8-track

*Some sources, including the notoriously unreliable Wikipedia, list the actual day of release as 9th. However, the industry standard at the time in the States was for new albums to be released on Mondays. July 9th was a Friday. As detailed in chapter four, *Record World* reported from a Warner Bros circular that the album was shipped on Friday 23rd July, which would have meant delivery to the stores for release on Monday 26th. Unless the date was brought forward, my hunch is that 26th July would have been the correct release date.

Reissues:
Warner Bros BS 2564, LP, 1973
Warner Bros BSK 2564, LP
Warner Bros 2564-2, CD, 1987
Rhino Records R2 75651, CD, 2000 *(25th Anniversary Edition)*
Friday Music FRM 2564, LP, 2010
Audio Fidelity AFZ 098, CD, 2010*

*The Audio Fidelity release was remastered from the original tapes by Steve Hoffman.

Rhino Records R1 35052, LP, 2016 *(180gram)*
Rhino Records RR1 2564, LP, 2019 *(purple vinyl)***

**These releases include 'Demon's Eye' instead of 'Strange Kind Of Woman'

UK
Original September releases:
Harvest, SHVL 793, LP
Harvest, TC-SHVL 793, cassette
Harvest, 8X SHVL 793, 8-track

*Some sources put the release date as 1st September, some as 15th. Both must be wrong as both these dates were Wednesdays and new releases always appeared on Fridays.

Reissues:
Fame FA 4130931, LP, 1984
Fame TC-FA 41 3093 4, cassette, 1984
Harvest EJ26 0344 0, 1985 *(picture disc)*
Harvest EMS 1255, LP, 1987
TC-EMS 1255, cassette, 1987
EMI CDP 746240 2, CD, 1989
EMI CDDEEPP 2, CD, 1996 *(25th Anniversary Edition)*
Harvest DEEPP 2, 2LP, 1996 *(25th Anniversary Edition)*
Parlophone 7243 8 53711 2 7, CD, 2013 *(25th Anniversary Edition)*
Harvest SHVL 793, LP, 2018 *(purple vinyl)*

Fireball reached number thirty-two on the US charts and number one on the UK charts.

Germany
Original releases
Harvest, 1C 062-92 726, LP, 1971
Harvest, 1C 244-92 726, cassette, 1971

Reissues:
Harvest 61 239, LP, 1971 *(Club Edition)*
Harvest 28 643-5, LP, 1971 *(Club Edition)*
Harvest 1C 072-92 726, LP, 1977
Harvest 1C 038 1575621, LP, 1984
EMI CDP 746240 2, CD, 1989
EMI 7243 8 53711 2 7, CD, 1996 *(25th Anniversary Edition)*
Harvest 7243 8 53711 1 0, 2LP, 1996 *(25th Anniversary Edition)*

Japan
Original releases
Warner Bros P-8092W, LP, July 1971

Reissues:
Warner Bros P-8092W, LP, 1974
Warner Bros P-10109W, LP, 1976
Warner Bros P-6506W, LP, 1981
Warner Bros 20P2-2604, CD, February 1989
Warner Bros TRZM-37, CD, 1994
Warner Bros WPCR-866, CD, 1996
Warner Bros WPCR-1140, CD, 1997 *(25th Anniversary Edition)*
Warner Bros WPCR-1565 CD, 1998
Warner Bros WPCR-10191 CD, 1999
Warner Bros WPCR-75034 CD, 2005
Warner Bros WPCR-12254 CD, 2006
Warner Bros WPCR-13111 CD, 2008
Warner Bros WPCR-78063 CD, 2013
Warner Bros WPCR-80216 CD, 2015

SINGLES

Strange Kind Of Woman / I'm Alone
Harvest HAR 5033, 12th February 1971, UK
Warner Bros 7493, May 1971, USA
Harvest 1C 006-92 301, February 1971, Germany
Warner Bros P-1054W, 1971, Japan

Fireball / Demon's Eye
Harvest HAR 5045, 29th October 1971, UK
Warner Bros 7528, September 1971, USA
Harvest 1C 006-92 988, 1971, Germany

Fireball / Anyone's Daughter
Warner Bros P-1089W, December 1971, Japan

Tour Dates

I have included all dates from the start of MkII, through to the release of *Machine Head*. Dates in grey, didn't happen.

1969

Thursday 10th July	Speakeasy Club, London, England
Friday 18th July	Coatham Hotel, Jazz Club, Redcar, England
Sunday 20th July	Mothers, Birmingham, England
Friday 25th July	Lyceum, London, England
Saturday 26th July	Klooks Kleek, Railway Hotel, West Hampstead, England
Monday 11th August	BBC Radio, Studio 2, London, England
	Broadcasted on Symonds On Sunday, *17th August*
Wednesday 13th August	Revolution Club, London, England
Friday 15th August	Mayfair Ballroom, Newcastle, England
Saturday 16th August	Rebecca's Club, Birmingham, England
Wednesday 20th August	London, Revolution Club, England
Friday 22nd August	Bilzen, Belgium (recorded for TV, *Tienerklanken*)
Saturday 23rd August	Paradiso, Amsterdam, Netherlands
Sunday 24th August	Paradiso, Amsterdam, Netherlands
Monday 25th August	Radio Bremen TV Bremen, Germany (*Beat-Club* Nr. 46)
Tuesday 26 August	Klooks Kleek, Railway Hotel, West Hampstead, England
Friday 29th August	Studio 1, BBC Radio, London, England
	Broadcasted on Stuart Henry Show, *7th September*
Friday 29th August	Lyceum, London, England
Saturday 30th August	Kent Pop Festival, Gravesend, Football Stadium, England
Tuesday 2nd September	Thames TV, London, England (*Today*)
Wednesday 3rd September	Cue Club, Gothenburg, Sweden
Friday 5th, September	Store Salen, Lund, Sweden
Saturday 6th September	Club Dynamite, Hotel Stevns, Store Heddinge, Denmark
Sunday 7th September	Fjordvilla, Roskilde, Denmark
Tuesday 9th September	Marquee, London, England
Friday 12th September	Queens Hall, Barnstaple, England
Saturday 13th September	Queens Hall, Narberth, England
Saturday 20th September	Winter Gardens, Malvern, England
Sunday 21st September	Coatham Hotel, Jazz Club, Redcar, England
Wednesday 24th September	Royal Albert Hall, London, England
	(*Concerto For Group & Orchestra*)
Saturday 27th September	College of Education, Nottingham, England
Sunday 28th September	Roundhouse, London, England
Tuesday 30th September	Studio 5 BBC Radio, London, England
	Broadcasted Stuart Henry Show, *13th-17th October*
Saturday 4th October	Casino, Montreux, Switzerland
Thursday 9th October	St. Moritz Augsburg, Germany
Friday 10th October	Stuttgart, Germany
Friday 10th October	Atlantic Bar, Stuttgart, Germany (aftershow jam session)
Saturday 11th October	Imperial College, London, England
Saturday 11th October	Pop & Blues Festival, Grugahalle, Essen, Germany
Sunday 12th October	Concertgebouw, Amsterdam, Netherlands
Tuesday 14th October	Musikhalle, Hamburg, Germany
Wednesday 22nd October	Baths Hall, Ipswich, England
Friday 24th October	Lyceum, London, England
Saturday 25th October	Winter Gardens, Weston-super-Mare, England
Thursday 30th October	University, Leeds, England
Friday 31st October	Studio 4, BBC Radio, London, England
	Broadcasted Stuart Henry Show, *9th November*
Saturday 1st November	Mayfair Ballroom, Bristol, England
Sunday 2nd November	Lyceum, London, England

Monday 3rd November	Roundhouse, London, England
Friday 7th November	King's Head, Romford, England
Saturday 8th November	Leas Cliff Hall, Folkstone, England
Monday 10th November	Pavilion, Bath, England
Thursday 13th November	Regency Theatre, Newport, Wales
Friday 14th November	Aston View, Birmingham, England
Saturday 15th November	Refectory, University, Leeds, England
Sunday 16th November	Kinema, Dunfermline, Scotland
Monday 17th November	Electric Garden, Glasgow, Scotland
Friday 21st November	Avery Hill College, Eltham, England
Saturday 22nd November	University, Bradford, England
Sunday 23rd November	Groovesville, Epping, England
Monday 24th November	Bennett Concert Hall, Birmingham, England
Friday 28th November	Civic Hall, Guildford, England
Saturday 29th November	Imperial College, London, England
Sunday 30th November	Roundhouse, London, England
Thursday 4th December	Assembly Hall, Worthing, England
Friday 5th December	Polytechnic, Sunderland, England
Saturday 6th December	U.M.I.S.T., University, Manchester, England
Sunday 7th December	St. George's Hall, Bradford, England
Tuesday 9th December	Keele University, Stafford, England
Wednesday 10th December	University College, London, England
Thursday 11th December	Royal Ballrooms, Boscombe, Bournemouth, England
Friday 12th December	Flamingo, Hereford, England
Monday 15th December	Cosmopolitan, Carlisle, England
Thursday 18th December	Flamingo, Redruth, England
Friday 19th December	Van Dyke Club, Plymouth, England
Saturday 20th December	The Village, Roundhouse, Dagenham, England
Sunday 21st December	Mothers, Birmingham, England
Sunday 28th December	Greyhound, Croydon, England

1970

Monday 5th January	Pavillon 8, Anciennes Halles, Paris, France
Tuesday 6th January	Assembly Hall, Worthing, England
Wednesday 10th January	University of Reading, England
Thursday 15th January	Amsterdam, Netherlands (*Doebidoe* ARVO TV Show)
Friday 16th January	Amsterdam, Netherlands (*Doebidoe* ARVO TV Show)
Monday 19th January	Civic Hall, Dunstable, England
Wednesday 21st January	Big Apple, Munich, Germany
Friday 23rd January	Central Hall, University of Lancaster, Lancaster, England
Saturday 24th January	The Curzon, Hatfield, England
Friday 30th January	Royal Albert Hall, London, England
Saturday 31st January	Lawns Centre, Cottenham, England
Tuesday 3rd February	Bremen TV, Germany
Friday 6th February	Technical College, Waltham Forest, England
Saturday 7th February	Union Hall, University, Leicester, England
Sunday 8th February	Mothers, Birmingham, England
Friday 13th February	University, Cardiff, Wales
Saturday 14th February	Free Trade Hall, Manchester, England
Sunday 15th February	Boat Club, Nottingham, England
Monday 16th February	King's Head, Romford, England
Thursday 19th February	Paris Theatre, London, England
	Broadcasted The Sunday Show, *BBC 22nd February*
Friday 20th February	Public Hall, Harris College, Preston, England
Saturday 21st February	St. Mary's College, Twickenham, England
Sunday 22nd February	Greyhound, Croydon, England
Monday 23rd February	Music Hall, Aberdeen, Scotland
Tuesday 24th February	Imperial College, London, England
Wednesday 25th February	Anson Rooms, University, Bristol, England
Friday 27th February	Tech Faculty Hall, Polytechnic, Leeds, England
Saturday 28th February	Philharmonic Hall, Liverpool, England
Wednesday 4th March	Volkshaus, Zürich, Switzerland

Friday 6th March	Tanzdiele Matte, Bern, Switzerland
Saturday 7th March	Verkehrshaus, Luzern, Switzerland
Friday 13th March	Winter Gardens, Blackpool, England
Saturday 14th March	Empress Ballroom, Winter Gardens, Weston-super-Mare, England
Sunday 15th March	Wake Arms, Groovesville, England
Tuesday 17th March	University, Exeter, England
Friday 20th March	Odeon Theatre, Edinburgh, Scotland
Saturday 21st March	Caird Hall, Dundee, Scotland
Sunday 22nd March	Kinema, Dunfermline, Scotland
Monday 23rd March	Music Hall, Aberdeen, Scotland
Tuesday 24th March	Electric Garden, Glasgow, Scotland
Wednesday 25th March	Town Hall, Hamilton, Scotland
Saturday 28th March	The Village, Roundhouse, Dagenham, England
Sunday 29th March	Ernst-Merck-Halle, Hamburg, Germany
Monday 30th March	Sportpalast, Berlin, Germany
Saturday 4th April	Sporthalle Deutz, Cologne, Germany
Monday 6th April	Konzerthaus, Vienna, Austria
Saturday 11th April	Central Hall, Chatham, England
Saturday 18th April	Technical College, Ewell, England
Tuesday 21st April	Maida Vale Studio 5, BBC Radio, London, England
	Broadcasted on Sounds Of The Seventies
Friday 24th April	Kings Hall, North Staffs Polytechnic, Stoke-on-Trent, England
Saturday 25th April	Bath, England
Friday 1st May	Art College, Brighton, England
Saturday 9th May	The Village, Roundhouse, Dagenham, England
Monday 11th May	De Montfort Hall, Leicester, England
Friday 15th May	Chelmsford, England
Saturday 16th May	Town Hall, Birmingham, England
Sunday 17th May	Colston Hall, Bristol, England
Monday 18th May	Civic Hall, Dunstable, England
Friday 22nd May	Dome, Brighton, England
Monday 25th May	Queen Elizabeth Hall London, England (two shows)
Thursday 28th May	Ostseehalle, Kiel, Germany
Friday 29th May	Neue Welt, Berlin, Germany
Saturday 30th May	Circus Krone Bau Munich, Germany
Sunday 31st May	Rosengarten, Mannheim, Germany (two shows)

Deep Purple In Rock* released in June 1970

Monday 1st June	Rheinhalle, Düsseldorf, Germany
Tuesday 2nd June	Großer Saal, Musikhalle, Hamburg, Germany (2 shows)
Saturday 6th June	Großer Sartory Saal, Cologne, Germany (2 shows)
Sunday 7th June	Circus Krone Bau, Munich, Germany
Monday 8th June	Festhalle Mustermesse, Basel, Switzerland
Tuesday 9th June	Stadthalle, Offenbach, Germany
Wednesday 10th June	Niedersachsenhalle, Hannover, Germany
Friday 12th June	Colonel Barefoot's Rockgarden, Twickenham, England
Sunday 14th June	Fairfield Hall, Croydon, England
Tuesday 16th June	Jesus College, Cambridge, England
Wednesday 17th June	Aberdeen, Grampian TV, Scotland (*Pop Scotch '70*)
Friday 19th June	John Dalton College, Manchester, England
Saturday 20th June	University College, Oxford, England
Sunday 21st June	Radstadion, Frankfurt am Main, Germany
Saturday 4th July	The Eyrie, Bedford, England
Sunday 5th July	Lyceum, London, England
Friday 10th July	Sportpark Soers (Reitstadion), Aachen, Germany
Saturday 11th July	Große Halle, Eissportstadion, Munich, Germany
Tuesday 14th July	Granada Studios, Manchester, England
	Broadcasted on Doing Their Thing, *21st August*
Tuesday 28th July	Queen Elisabeth Hall, London, England
	Edited 'Mandrake Root' broadcasted on
	London Weekend TV, South Bank Summer, *5th September*

Friday 31st July	Mayfair Newcastle, England
Saturday 1st August	Progressive Music Festival, Chateau de Saint-Pons, France
Saturday 8th August	Stade Municipal, Saint Raphael, France
Sunday 9th August	Plumpton, Racecourse, 10 NJF Festival - England
Saturday 15th August	Island Groove Park Stampede & Rodeo Arena, Greeley, Colorado, USA
Sunday 16th August	Bullfrog Music Festival Estacada, Bullfrog, Oregon, USA
?? August	Houston, Texas, USA
?? August	Pepperland, San Rafael, California, USA
Saturday 22nd August	Ballroom, The Terrace, Salt Lake City, Utah, USA
Tuesday 25th August	Hollywood Bowl, Los Angeles, California, USA
	Concerto for Group and Orchestra with The L. A. Philharmonic
Friday 28th August	Jam Factory San Antonio, Texas, USA (2 shows)
	(Blackmore took ill. Christopher Cross replaced him for the second show)
Saturday 29th August	Civic Auditorium, Albuquerque, New Mexico, USA
Sunday 30th August	Civic Auditorium, Pasadena, California, USA
Sunday 6th September	Festival, Arras, France
Wednesday 9th September	BBC TV, Lime Grove Studio, London, England
	'Black Night' broadcasted on Top of the Pops, *10th September*
Thursday 17th September	Royal Festival Hall, London, England
	Premiere of the Gemini Suite. Broadcasted on BBC Radio 2, South Bank Pops
Wednesday 23rd September	Studio T1, BBC Radio, London, England
Friday 25th September	Odeon, Romford, England
Friday 2nd October	U.W.I.S.T., University, Cardiff, Wales
Saturday 3rd October	University of Southampton, England
Sunday 4th October	Lausanne, Switzerland (unconfimed)
Tuesday 6th October	University Refectory, Leeds, England
Thursday 8th October	La Taverne de L'Olympia, Paris, France
	Broadcasted on Pop Deux
Saturday 10th October	University of Sheffield, England
Monday 12th October	Tiffany's, Edinburgh, Scotland
Tuesday 13th October	Tiffany's, Glasgow, Scotland
Wednesday 14th October	Concert Hall, Aberdeen, Scotland
Friday 15th October	Caird Hall, Dundee, Scotland
Saturday 16th October	Top Rank Suite, Sunderland, England
Sunday 17th October	University of Manchester, England
Wednesday 21st October	Top Rank, Swansea, Wales
Sunday 25th October	Theatre du Huitieme, Lyon, France
Monday 26th October	Maison de la Culture, Chambery, France
Tuesday 27th October	Maison des Arts, Sochaux, France
Wednesday 28th October	Maison de la Culture, Mulhouse, France
Friday 30th October	Maison de la Culture, Le Havre, France
Saturday 31st October	Club Piblokto, Dourges, France
Sunday 1st November	Olympia, Paris, France
Sunday 1st November	Gibus Club, Paris, France
Monday 2nd November	Cinema-Theatre, Elbeuf, France
Tuesday 3rd November	Cinema Le Celtic, Brest, France
Friday 6th November	Winter Gardens, Bournemouth, England
Saturday 7th November	Dreamland, Margate, England
Wednesday 11th November	Club 7, Njardhallen, Oslo, Norway
Thursday 12th November	Konserthus, Stockholm, Sweden
	Broadcasted by Swedish Radio, Tonkraft. *Subsequently released*
Saturday 14th November	K.B. Hallen, Copenhagen, Denmark
Sunday 15th November	Konserthus, Gothenburg, Sweden
Monday 16th November	Fyens Forum, Odense, Denmark
Wednesday 18th November	St George's Hall, Liverpool, England
Thursday 19th November	Belle Vue, Manchester, England
Friday 20th November	City Hall, Hull, England
Saturday 21st November	University College, London, England
Sunday 22nd November	Fairfield Hall, Croydon, England

Monday 23rd November   Civic Hall, Wolverhampton, England
Tuesday 24th November   St. Georges Hall, Bradford, England
Friday 27th November   Stadthalle, Offenbach, Germany
Saturday 28th November   Neue Universität, Heidelberg, Germany
Sunday 29th November   Rheinhalle, Düsseldorf, Germany
Monday 30th November   Mercatorhalle, Duisburg, Germany
Tuesday 1st December   Niedersachsenhalle, Hannover, Germany
Wednesday 2nd December   Planten un Blomen, Halle B, Hamburg, Germany
Thursday 3rd December   Planten un Blomen, Halle B, Hamburg, Germany
Friday 4th December   Halle Münsterland, Münster, Germany
Saturday 5th December   Circus Krone Bau, Munich, Germany
Sunday 6th December   Saarlandhalle, Saarbrücken, Germany
Monday 7th December   Meistersingerhalle, Nürnberg, Germany
Tuesday 8th December   Schützenhalle, Lüdenscheid, Germany (without Ritchie)
Wednesday 9th December   Stadthalle, Kassel, Germany
Wednesday 9th December   Basel, Switzerland
Thursday 10th December   Zurich, Switzerland
Friday 11th December   Huttenhalle, Würzburg, Germany
Saturday 12th December   Messegelände Killesberg, Stuttgart, Germany
Thursday 17th December   Dome, Brighton, England
Saturday 19th December   The Village, Roundhouse, Dagenham, England

1971

Friday 1st January   De Doelen, Rotterdam, Netherlands
Saturday 2nd January   Rai, Amsterdam, Netherlands
Friday 29th January   Town Hall, Leeds, England
Saturday 30th January   Philharmonic Hall, Liverpool, England
Monday 1st February   Royal Albert Hall, London, England
Friday 5th February   ABC Cinema, Kingston upon Hull, England
Saturday 6th February   City Hall, Sheffield, England
Sunday 7th February   Winter Gardens, Bournemouth, England
Monday 8th February   Guildhall, Southampton, England
Tuesday 9th February   Guildhall, Portsmouth, England
Friday 12th February   Town Hall, Birmingham, England
Saturday 13th February   Colston Hall, Bristol, England
Sunday 14th February   ABC Cinema, Plymouth, England
Friday 19th February   Belle Vue, Manchester, England
Saturday 20th February   City Hall, Newcastle, England
Sunday 21st February   Coventry Theatre, England
Monday 22nd February   Orchid, Purley, England
Thursday 25th February   De Montfort Hall, Leicester, England
Saturday 27th February   Big Apple, Brighton, England
Friday 5th March   Green's Playhouse, Glasgow, Scotland
Saturday 6th March   Empire Theatre, Edinburgh, Scotland
Sunday 7th March   Caird Hall, Dundee, Scotland
Monday 8th March   Music Hall, Aberdeen, Scotland
Saturday 3rd April   Deutschlandhalle, Berlin, Germany
Wednesday 7th April   Weser-Ems-Halle, Oldenburg, Germany
Thursday 8th April   Grugahalle, Essen, Germany
Friday 10th April   Stadthalle, Offenbach, Germany
Saturday 11th April   Planten un Blomen, Halle C, Hamburg, Germany
?? April   Olympiahalle, Munich, Germany
Friday 16th April   Casino, Montreux, Switzerland (filmed by Swiss TV)
Saturday 17th April   Casino, Montreux, Switzerland
Monday 19th April   Palais des Beaux-Arts, Brussels, Belgium
Wednesday 21st April   Konserthus, Stockholm, Sweden
Thursday 22nd April   Konserthus, Stockholm, Sweden
Friday 23rd April   K.B. Hallen, Copenhagen, Denmark
Saturday 24th April   Vejlby-Risskov Hallen, Aarhus, Denmark
Sunday 25th April   Aalborghallen, Aalborg, Denmark
Monday 26th April   Njardhallen, Oslo, Norway
Friday 30th April   Roundhouse, London, England

Thursday 6th May	Beatty Park Aquatic Centre, Perth, Australia
Friday 7th May	Festival Hall, Melbourne, Australia
Saturday 8th May	Apollo Stadium, Adelaide, Australia
Sunday 9th May	Randwick Racecourse, Sydney, Australia
Monday 10th May	Festival Hall, Brisbane, Australia
Friday 21st May	Deutschlandhalle, Berlin, Germany
Tuesday 25th May	Palasport, Rome, Italy (2 shows)
Thursday 27th May	Palasport, Bologna, Italy (2 shows)
Saturday 29th May	Eishalle, Wetzikon, Switzerland
Sunday 6th June	Stade Achille Hammerel, Bonneweg, Luxembourg
Friday 18th June	Laugardalshöllinni, Reykjavik, Iceland
Thursday 24th June	Kinetic Circus, Birmingham, England
Friday 25th June	Mayfair, Newcastle, England
Saturday 26 June	Italian TV, Italy
Sunday 27th June	Italian TV, Italy

Fireball* was released in the US in July 1971

Friday 2nd July	St. Lawrence Market, Toronto, Ontario, Canada
Saturday 3rd July	Gilligan's, Buffalo, New York, USA
Sunday 4th July	Overton Park, Memphis, Tennessee, USA
Tuesday 6th July	Forum, Hamilton, Ontario, Canada
Wednesday 7th July	Wonderland Gardens, London, Ontario, Canada
Thursday 8th July	Philharmonic Hall, New York City, New York, USA
Friday 9th July	Spectrum, Philadelphia, Pennsylvania, USA
Saturday 10th July	Public Hall, Cleveland, Ohio, USA
Sunday 11th July	Minneapolis Auditorium, Minneapolis, Minnesota, USA
Wednesday 14th July	Bruce Hall, Milwaukee, Wisconsin, USA
Friday 16th July	Syria Mosque, Pittsburgh, Pennsylvania, USA
Saturday 17th July	Hara Arena, Dayton, Ohio, USA
Sunday 18th July	Sports Arena, Toledo, Ohio, USA
Tuesday 20th July	Auditorium Theatre, Chicago, Illinois, USA
Wednesday 21st July	Auditorium Theatre, Chicago, Illinois, USA
Friday 23rd July	Pirates World, Dania, Florida, USA
Saturday 24th July	Orlando Sport Stadium, Orlando, Florida, USA
Sunday 25th July	Warehouse, New Orleans, Lousiana, USA
Tuesday 27th July	Municipal Auditorium, San Antonio, Texas, USA
Wednesday 28th July	Sam Houston Coliseum, Houston, Texas, USA
Thursday 29th July	Sgt. Pepper's, Wichita, Kansas, USA
Friday 30th July	Long Beach Arena, Los Angeles, California, USA
Saturday 31st July	Salt Palace, Salt Lake City, Utah, USA

Fireball* was released in the UK in September 1971

Wednesday 1st September	IFA Messegelände, Berlin, Germany
	Broadcasted on SFB TV Music Today, *22nd September*
Saturday 4th September	Stadthalle, Vienna, Austria
Sunday 5th September	Rheinhalbinsel, Speyer, Germany
Monday 13th September	Guildhall, Portsmouth, England
Sunday 19th September	De Montfort Hall, Leicester, England
Wednesday 22nd September	Free Trade Hall, Manchester, England
Thursday 23rd September	Philharmonic Hall, Liverpool, England
Friday 24th September	Green's Playhouse, Glasgow, Scotland
Saturday 25th September	Empire Theatre, Edinburgh, Scotland
Sunday 26th September	City Hall, Newcastle, England
Wednesday 29th September	Winter Gardens, Bournemouth, England
Thursday 30th September	Royal Albert Hall, London, England
Tuesday 5th October	City Hall, Sheffield, England
Sunday 10th October	Coventry Theatre, England
Monday 11th October	Guildhall, Southampton, England
Friday 22nd October	Felt Forum, New York City, New York, USA
Saturday 23rd October	William and Mary Hall, Williamsburg, Virginia, USA

Sunday 24th October	Auditorium Theatre, Chicago, Illinois, USA
	Without Ian Gillan who went down with hepatitis.
	Glover did the vocals. The rest of the tour was cancelled.
Monday 25th October	Hamilton, Ontario, Canada
Saturday 30th October	Vets Memorial, Columbus, Ohio, USA
Sunday 31st October	Grand Valley State College, Allendale, Michigan, USA
Wednesday 3rd November	Music Hall, Boston, Massachusetts, USA
Saturday 6th November	Sportatorium, Hollywood, Florida, USA
Sunday 7th November	St. Petersburg Bayfront Center, Tampa, Florida, USA
Tuesday 9th November	Syria Mosque, Pittsburgh, Pennsylvania, USA
Wednesday 10th November	Memorial Auditiorim, Kansas City, Kansas, USA
Friday 19th November	Henry Lewitt Arena, Wichita, Kansas, USA
Saturday 20th November	Ford Auditorium, Detroit, Michigan, USA
Sunday 21st November	Bangor, Maine, USA
Wednesday 24th November	Academy of Music, New York City, New York, USA
Wednesday 15th December	BBC TV Studios, London, England
	'Fireball' broadcasted on Top of the Pops, *16th December*
Thursday 30th December	Stockholm, Sweden (unconfirmed)

1972

Tuesday 4th January	Konzerthalle, Munich, Germany
	Planned second performance of the Gemini Suite
Wednesday 5th January	Hamburg, Germany
Thursday 13th January	Sportatorium, Hollywood, Florida, USA
Friday 14th January	Curtis Hixon Hall, Tampa, Florida, USA
Saturday 15th January	Littlejohn Coliseum, Clemson, South Carolina, USA
Sunday 16th January	Cumberland, Fayetteville, North Carolina, USA
Monday 17th January	Memorial Auditorium, Buffalo, New York, USA
Wednesday 19th January	Ford Auditorium Detroit, Michigan, USA
Thursday 20th January	The Forum, Montreal, Quebec, Canada
Friday 21st January	Metropolitan Sports Center, Bloomington, Minnesota, USA
Saturday 22nd January	Auditorium Theatre, Chicago, Illinois, USA
Sunday 23rd January	Auditorium Theatre, Chicago, Illinois, USA
Monday 24th January	Kiel Stadium, St. Louis, Missouri, USA
Wednesday 26th January	Wichita Forum, Wichita, Kansas, USA
Friday 28th January	Swing Auditorium, San Bernardino, California, USA
Saturday 29th January	County Fairgrounds, Santa Clara, California, USA
Sunday 30th January	Long Beach Auditorium, Long Beach, California, USA
Monday 31st January	State College Gym, Boise, Idaho, USA
Saturday 5th February	Oberschwabenhalle, Ravensburg, Germany
Monday 7th February	Halle Münsterland, Münster, Germany
Wednesday 9th February	Hannover, Niedersachsenhalle Germany
Thursday 10th February	Sporthalle, Böblingen, Germany
Friday 11th February	Oststadthalle, Karlsruhe, Germany
Saturday 12th February	Grugahalle, Essen, Germany
Sunday 13th February	Sporthalle, Augsburg, Germany
Saturday 19th February	The Village, Roundhouse, Dagenham, England
Sunday 20th February	Civic Hall, Wolverhampton, England
Tuesday 22nd February	Orchid, Purley, England
Saturday 26th February	Old Messuhalli, Helsinki, Finland
Tuesday 29th February	Scandinavium, Gothenburg, Sweden
Wednesday 1st March	K.B. Hallen Copenhagen, Denmark
	Broadcasted by Danmarks Radio TV
Friday 3rd March	Fyens Forum / Fyns Forum, Odense, Denmark
Saturday 4th March	Vejlby-Risskov Hallen, Aarhus, Denmark
Thursday 9th March	Paris Theatre, London, England
	Broadcasted by the BBC, Sounds of the Seventies, *18th March*
Sunday 12th March	Fairfield Hall, Croydon, England
Friday 17th March	Memorial Hall, Kansas City, Kansas, USA
Saturday 18th March	Municipal Auditorium, Austin, Texas, USA

Sunday 19th March	Sam Houston Coliseum, Houston, Texas, USA
Monday 20th March	International Building, Oklahoma City, Oklahoma, USA
Thursday 23rd March	Madison County Coliseum, Huntsville, Alabama, USA
Friday 24th March	West Palm Beach Auditorium, Florida, USA
Saturday 25th March	Jacksonville Coliseum, Jacksonville, Florida, USA
Sunday 26th March	Charlotte, North Carolina, USA
Tuesday 28th March	Ritz Theatre, Staten Island, New York, USA
Wednesday 29th March	Ritz Theatre, Staten Island, New York, USA
Thursday 30th March	Ford Auditorium, Detroit, Michigan, USA
Friday 31st March	Flint, Michigan, USA DP played 4 songs, without Ritchie
Saturday 1st April	Vet's Memorial Auditorium, Columbus, Ohio, USA
Sunday 2nd April	Ford Auditorium, Detroit, Michigan, USA
Monday 3rd April	Cenvention Centre, Louisville, Kentucky, USA
Tuesday 4th April	Syria Mosque, Pittsburgh, Pennsylvania, USA
Thursday 6th April	Colisee de Quebec, Quebec City, Quebec, Canada
	Without Ritchie Blackmore who went down with hepatitis.
	Randy California stepped in. The rest of the tour was cancelled.
Saturday 8th April	Hara Arena, Dayton, Ohio, USA
Tuesday 11th April	Civic Theatre, Akron, Ohio, USA
Wednesday 12th April	Performing Arts Centre, Milwaukee, Wisconsin, USA
Friday 14th April	Community Theatre, Berkeley, California, USA
Saturday 15th April	Convention Centre, Anaheim, California, USA
Sunday 16th April	Convention Hall, San Diego, California, USA
Thursday 20th April	PNE Garden Auditorium, Vancouver, BC, Canada
Friday 21st April	Armory Auditorium, Salem, Oregon, USA
Sunday 23rd April	Civic Auditorium, Honolulu, Hawaii, USA
Thursday 11th May	Kosei Nenkin Kaikan, Osaka, Japan
Friday 12th May	Kosei Nenkin Kaikan, Osaka, Japan
Tuesday 16th May	Budokan, Tokyo, Japan
Thursday 25th May	Ford Auditorium, Detroit, Michigan, USA
Friday 26th May	Hara Arena, Dayton, Ohio, USA
Sunday 28th May	Public Hall, Cleveland, Ohio, USA
Tuesday 30th May	Edmonton Gardens, Edmonton, Alberta, Canada

Machine Head* was released in May 1972

In-depth Series

The In-depth series was launched in March 2021 with four titles. Each book takes an in-depth look at an album; the history behind it; the story about its creation; the songs, as well as detailed discographies listing release variations around the world. The series will tackle albums that are considered to be classics amongst the fan bases, as well as some albums deemed to be "difficult" or controversial; shining new light on them, following reappraisal by the authors.

Titles to date:
Jethro Tull - Thick As A Brick   978-1-912782-57-4
Tears For Fears - The Hurting   978-1-912782-58-1
Kate Bush - The Kick Inside   978-1-912782-59-8
Deep Purple - Stormbringer   978-1-912782-60-4
Emerson Lake & Palmer - Pictures At An Exhibition 978-1-912782-67-3
Korn - Follow The Leader   978-1-912782-68-0
Elvis Costello - This Year's Model   978-1-912782-69-7
Kate Bush - The Dreaming   978-1-912782-70-3
Jethro Tull - Minstrel In The Gallery   978-1-912782-81-9
Deep Purple - Fireball   978-1-912782-82-6
Deep Purple - Slaves And Masters   978-1-912782-83-3

Forthcoming:
Talking Heads - Remain In Light
Jethro Tull - Heavy Horses
Rainbow - Straight Between The Eyes
The Stranglers - La Folie
Alice Cooper - Love It To Death